DATE DUE

MODERNIZING AMERICA

Action Papers
of National Purpose

Foreword by
STAN MUSIAL

Edited by
JOHN McCOOK ROOTS

PACE PUBLICATIONS
Los Angeles

First Printing, December 1965
Second Printing, March 1966

CONTENTS

FOREWORD

by

Stan Musial

*Special Consultant on Physical Fitness to the President
of the United States; Vice-President, St. Louis Cardinals*

I saw Moral Re-Armament in action at Mackinac Island
this summer. I shall always remember what I saw. Through
its training program it is giving youth an aim and purpose
for their lives and making them into responsible and patriotic
citizens.

I wish I could pass on to all of our youth, and specially
our athletes, the great benefits of this sort of training. I hope
that our leaders in all walks of life, from the Government
on down, will actively participate in it.

With the responsibilities we face today, Americans need
to learn more than just a vocation or profession. We need
to learn how to deal with people. For people are still our
most important asset, both here at home and wherever we
go in the world.

This book, written by some of the ablest men in America
and abroad, represents just about the best thinking I know
on issues of the day. I hope it will be widely read by students
and faculty, by business men and churchmen, by labor and
industry, and by all who are active in civic and governmental
affairs. Particularly I hope it will be read by my colleagues
whom I know so well in the world of sport.

Stan Musial

St. Louis
December, 1965

INTRODUCTION

T HE WORLD IS WAITING for something new to come out of
America. Awed a little by our technical achievements, critical
often of our operating style, jealous perhaps of our wealth, confused certainly as to our aims and purposes, two thousand million
human beings are nevertheless sparked by a hope that somehow,
sometime, this fabled land of opportunity may produce for all
men everywhere the key to a new age.

The great question of the century—greater by far than the inten-
tions of Red China, the succession in the Kremlin, or the Moscow-
Peking split—is whether or not America will fulfil that hope and
produce the key.

We are a nation whose wealth, power and generosity are legendary, but whose armory of skills is in certain vital respects sadly
out of date.

We boast the most modern educational system on earth but are
at our wits end how to communicate with our own sons and daughters. We enact an historic civil rights bill, but are helpless before
the storm of racial hate unleashed at Watts. We erect a brilliant
system of alliances, yet are deeply divided from our oldest ally and
barely on speaking terms with others. We give a hundred billion
dollars in foreign aid, only to see our libraries burnt and our envoys
spat upon, mainly because we have not yet learned the art of giving
other nations a great idea and partnership in a common task.

The truth is that America needs a new dimension of domestic
and foreign policy, directed to new goals, and implemented by men
with new motives and new skills, to meet new problems never
before faced by any generation in the history of the Republic.

In the chapters that follow, made up of addresses delivered at
the Demonstration for Modernizing America at Mackinac Island,
Michigan last summer, the reader will find heartening evidence
that something new is indeed beginning to come out of this country
that can bring the nation up to date.

He will discover guide-lines for new policies, and how to produce the new men to implement them. He will find evidence of

what such new men have already achieved towards turning the tide of events. He will gain salutary insights into where and how things have gone wrong in the past, and breath-taking vistas of what the future may hold. He will discern a blueprint for modernizing America.

Professor Ramakrishna Vaitheswaran, a brilliant Indian intellectual and former Communist guerrilla, sums up in Chapter 19 the impression of those from abroad who attended this center for the training of youth in the disciplines and purposes of free democracy. He writes of the Demonstration:

"The whole world is here—Asia, Europe, Africa, Latin America and Australia as well as every part of the United States and Canada. They come worried about this nation, perhaps even resentful of her leadership, certainly anxious that they should help this country fulfil her world responsibility better. But where they anticipate arrogance, they find a ready listener and where they expect resistance, they find respect. It comes as a pleasant shock that the United States of America, tired of the aimlessness of affluence, frustrated by the senseless indulgence and wanton destruction of a sick generation, and defeated by the failure to evoke much enthusiasm in the nation or abroad for its world responsibility, is turning to what a friend of mine called 'pure undiluted Moral Re-Armament.' "

What does the world hope for from America? Economic aid, certainly. Military aid where needed, certainly. But most of all, this book makes clear, the world hopes to learn how to lay hold on those elusive intangibles that are the true source of national strength and greatness.

The world wants from America not pacifism but patriotism; not cynicism, division and aimlessness, but the secret of unity, faith and a giant purpose. They want an America that knows *why* as well as one that knows *how*. They want not only freedom from Communism, but an idea superior to Communism; not simply arms to halt an aggressor, but also an ideology to win, change and re-direct him.

In these pages the reader will also find an answer to other burning questions of the day.

In *Plan for China* (Ch. 3) Rajmohan Gandhi, grandson of the Mahatma and leader of India's youth, explains why U.S. foreign aid has won so few friends, and suggests concrete remedies that only a warm and imaginative admirer of this country could conceive.

In *Gold Medals and Red Russians* (Ch. 2) Richard Wailes gives a graphic report of his encounter with Soviet representatives at the

Tokyo Games, and in *What Makes a Revolutionary* (Ch. 17) his colleague John Sayre recalls a dramatic dialogue with eight Brazilian adherents of Fidel Castro.

In Chapter 16 an expert on Eastern Europe proposes ways in which our Cultural Exchange program could be employed to breach the Iron Curtain, while in Chapter 9 a former guerrilla leader gives a penetrating analysis of the American position in Vietnam, and the way out.

Those concerned with Africa will find in Chapter 5 an inside view of the Congo, and in *Continent of the Future* (Ch. 15) an illuminating survey of the richly varied complex of states and cultures between Cairo and the Cape. The writers' revolutionary concepts of race and national purpose suggest a new policy dimension in which hitherto irreconcilable antagonisms might at last be resolved.

One of the untold sagas behind Latin America's most notable national revolution is revealed by Alberto Kowarick of Brazil in Chapter 7, and Conrad Hunte in Chapter 12 gives a famous sportsman's recipe for out-revolutionizing Cuba in the Caribbean.

Running through the book are reminders of the glittering opportunity which faces America and the free nations in the period of ideological decline now slowly engulfing the Sino-Soviet bloc.

Of special interest is Morris Martin's analysis in Chapter 4 of the philosophy of Frank Buchman, American initiator of Moral Re-Armament. "The most dedicated Communist," he writes, "must divide the world in uniting his section of it. The most selfless nationalist must split continents while giving all for his nation. The true patriot, said Frank Buchman, gives his life to bring his nation and its leaders under God's control."

Training at the Mackinac Island Demonstration was meant to produce, and did, concrete plans and productions to forward America's world task. Chief among these was the traveling hit-show *Sing-Out '65,* conceived by the Colwell Brothers of California and directed by Henry Cass of London, with a multi-racial cast ranging from 130 to 180 representing 68 colleges and high schools in 41 states. Concluding the book is a special picture feature—*Torch of Freedom*—portraying the highlights of *Sing-Out '65's* current international tour.

Vibrant with the color and pace of the "go" generation and manned by a new, tough student breed resolved to supplant our pacifist beatniks as the prototype of American youth, this stirring musical spectacular is putting fresh militancy and contagion into the country's ideals and recreating Uncle Sam's image abroad. Its fast-moving repertoire of swing tunes is steeped in patriotic feeling but carries a universal theme. Already the show has been acclaimed by thousands, from Washington and Watts to Tokyo and Seoul, as a spearhead of the nation's positive answer to the Communist creed, and its company of dedicated youth as young America's first expeditionary force in the war of ideas.

Said a Latin American diplomat just returned from a visit to Eastern Europe, "I have always hoped to see the show-conscious U.S.A. dramatize the best of her traditional values as effectively as these Communist countries do. Now I have seen it."

Most remarkable result of the summer was the discovery among the 7,000 youth in training at Mackinac that, contrary to popular belief, young America has in fact a burning desire to tackle the world tasks which so manifestly need tackling. They respect age and experience and honor the manifold achievements of the past. But they do not intend to be dominated any longer by the built-in pattern of prejudices, cynicisms, complacencies and shibboleths of an older generation who they feel have failed to learn the lessons of history or come to grips with the real issues of life. Their declaration, reported in Chapter 19, forms a moving manifesto of faith in this land and in her future.

"We believe in America," they write. "We want a great country —respected and followed because of her great purpose and way of life. Our generation is going to explode the hate, fear and greed that blocks the progress of humanity. We want to race to take up our responsibilities. We will not remain comfortable and quiet while millions the world over have too little to eat, millions are deprived of their just freedom, and millions in our own country are starved of any purpose for which to live."

It will be evident I think, to the discerning reader, that in the authors of these chapters, and notably in the young Americans to whom they speak and who themselves speak in *Sing-Out '65,* a new type of free man is indeed arising with the will to turn the tide of history. As Professor Vaitheswaran states in concluding his *Key to America's World Role:* "From Mackinac is emerging a strategy to change continents—and the people who will do it."

JOHN McCOOK ROOTS

9

J. BLANTON BELK, JR., *of Richmond, Virginia, Director of Moral Re-Armament in the United States, was Chairman of the Demonstration for Modernizing America at Mackinac Island in 1965 and gave the key-note address. After attending Davidson College and the University of North Carolina, he enlisted in the Navy during World War II and served as an officer with a PC Boat in the Pacific. As a close colleague of the late Dr. Frank Buchman and Peter Howard he has an intimate knowledge of men and affairs in many parts of the world. Mr. Belk is 40 years old, married, with one daughter, and makes his home in Tucson, Arizona.*

1

MODERNIZING AMERICA

by

J. Blanton Belk, Jr.

O UR PURPOSE here is to produce modern men and women—men
and women with a world aim who demonstrate in their lives
the answers to the knottiest problems of our time. The modernization of man is the unlimited frontier for this generation to explore.

We called this summer a Demonstration because an idea, to be
heeded, must be demonstrated. To be noticed, it must produce
facts and figures. To be felt, it must have pragmatic plans for
Vietnam, Santo Domingo, poverty, class and race, war, juvenile
delinquency, world Communism, corruption, dope and division.
To be relevant, it must tackle the most difficult problem in the life
of every man, woman, child—and nation.

That is exactly what Moral Re-Armament is doing.

Last fall President Johnson launched the idea of "The Great
Society" at the University of Michigan. Youth from this conference
here in Michigan went out and began building the great society.
These young men and women were realists. They knew that any
great society had to begin with greatness in men. They were not
content to take the cheap course of sitting and finger-pointing.

Finger-pointing has become a national pastime—youth pointing
at age, age at youth, students at professors, professors at students,
black at white, white at black, Republicans at Democrats, Democrats at Republicans. It is the mark of an immature people. As a
people and as a nation we have got to grow up.

Sometimes others see us more clearly than we see ourselves. A
Russian philosopher, after lecturing in this country, was quoted
last week as saying, "The impotence of American philosophy is its
failure to oppose Marxism with a positive social ideal capable of

11

inspiring the masses, and with a moral conception of the future."

What that Russian does not know is that last summer hundreds of young Americans went out from here with a conception far bigger than anything Marxism has to offer.

You went out of here last summer to Appalachia, to the South, to the Southwest, to the West and East Coasts, from Maine to Florida and across Canada. Twenty-seven assemblies for youth have been held around the world inspired by your conference.

Think of Appalachia. During this year 40,000 students of West Virginia have heard about MRA at school assemblies throughout the state. The youngest daughter of the Emperor of Japan recently went to see what was going on. A busload of students from the mining valleys there recently travelled to Washington, D.C. to call on their Senators and Congressmen and other government officials. A young girl from McDowell County, West Virginia, spoke:

"With 18 people in a four-room house, it can get kind of cluttered. Moral Re-Armament came into our home. I was honest with my mother about things she didn't know. Since then she has stopped drinking. Our family is united. Now money from the government is used for food and other things we need."

One Congressman said, "You must speak to all the Senators and Congressmen of the seven Appalachian states. We should be financing your work in Appalachia." The Mayor of Charleston, W. Va., wrote a check to help them come to Mackinac.

Appalachia could export to the four corners of the earth an answer for the millions who live in economic poverty, and also for the millions who suffer from poverty of purpose.

They say we are in for a long, hot, simmering summer of racial violence. There is no need for it if we multiply this demonstration swiftly enough. You have demonstrated that it works in both South and North. I think of Judge Austin T. Walden of Atlanta, Georgia, first Negro municipal judge in the South since Reconstruction, when white and black youth from last year's conference reported to him. He said, and I quote from the front page of the *Atlanta Daily World,* "Moral Re-Armament is the blueprint of the new society we are all trying to build."

Senator Robert Kennedy just received a delegation of high school and college leaders, white and black, from Manhattan, Harlem and the Bronx. They told the Senator how at Mayor Wagner's request they had met with the Youth Commissioners of the City. Five times they broadcast on "Harlem, U.S.A." They told of practical steps they were taking to attack delinquency, dope, apathy, cheating and lack of purpose in New York high schools.

Isn't it time Americans—both black and white—stopped fighting each other and started tackling together these basic problems which face all of us regardless of the color of our skin?

The son of a Wall Street banker and a Negro student civil-rights leader from the South went together to Brazil this winter. They spoke in 37 colleges and universities. Everywhere they met a tumultuous response from the students who said, "What you tell us is more revolutionary than Castro, or Red China. If America lived this way, the whole world would listen and follow."

A young girl trained here last summer wrote a letter to Mrs. Lyndon Johnson. She comes from a broken home. She told Mrs. Johnson how her bitterness had been cured at Mackinac and how she found a new purpose for her life. She said, "I am one of 14 million American youth from broken homes. I want to erase that national image and create a new one of sound homes." She added that these 14 million youth, with the answer she had found, could become an army to build unity of purpose back into the nation.

Now a word about the universities, colleges and high schools of America. The hottest news has been the response in universities across the land to two Olympic Gold Medal winners, John Sayre and "Rusty" Wailes. Last year they trained in the thinking and standards of Mackinac the U.S. Olympic team that went to Japan and returned covered with Gold Medals.

The Soviet athletes met Sayre and Wailes and said to them, "We need your kind of revolution in Russia. You must come." The Russians may understand more clearly than some of us Americans the need for the modernization of man as the next step for the Communist and non-Communist world. In a recent dispatch from Moscow an American correspondent wrote, "A campaign is under way in the Soviet Union for more humaneness, kindness, and tact in human relations . . . As far as the Party is concerned, it represents an effort toward moral rebirth which duplicates in a sober way certain traits of the Moral Re-Armament movement in the West."

Sayre and Wailes have spoken on a hundred campuses in the past two-and-a-half months, from Berkeley to Mississippi, from the Air Force Academy to Michigan. They have had standing ovations.

Speaking last month on the Berkeley campus of the University of California, John Sayre said, "In nations like Vietnam it is necessary to defend freedom with military might. I am not a pacifist.

If it is necessary to defend freedom and faith with arms, I will do so. But America must give to North and South Vietnam and China an idea big enough so that all can change where they need to and move ahead to meet the needs of the millions of Asia for food, work and an idea that satisfies."

We are planning to mobilize the 9,000 high schools of the country, and "Rusty" Wailes goes to Florida today to speak to the high school principals of that state.

This brings us to the American Indian. Last summer you were 200. At Christmas in Albuquerque you were 750. This summer you will be over one thousand and you already have 48 tribes represented here. In Latin America a man in Quito, Ecuador, said to me, "The most significant event of 1965 in North America is the American Indian starting to speak out and call for the moral re-armament of America."

There is one man who stands here among us in spirit as we open this conference. He is Peter Howard. The last major speech he made in this country was at your conference in Albuquerque at Christmas. He said something then which I would like to read:

"What is needed is a prophet voice from a prophet people that the whole world will heed. I tell you solemnly, I believe it is God's plan now for the Indian peoples of this country to become such a voice. They can speak unitedly and with passion, but also with compassion, to America and the entire world.

"That would be a voice worthy of the high tradition of the original inhabitants of this land. It would be a voice that the Great Spirit, God, Christ, longs to hear from the Indian people. For my part, if you will let me do it with you, I will do it till the end of my days. I want to serve, I want to fight, I want to battle, and for me and for those of us who decide, there will be no turning back."

This is your hour to speak, and I hope out of this summer you will produce a great Indian pageant—a world weapon. Do it your own unique way, symbolizing the modernizing of men and nations.

The eyes of the world are on this conference. I was recently with former Chancellor Adenauer. When I told him young America was responding to Moral Re-Armament he said, "That is the finest news I have heard from America." Then he pointed his 89-year-old finger at me and said urgently, "You must get to General de Gaulle. You must give him this news of a new America." Dr. Adenauer knows the power of MRA to unite divided nations. He has just written a letter saying, "I believe your Mackinac Demonstration will strengthen the fabric of world peace."

I have recently returned from a visit to Japan. In five days I had conferences with Mr. Sato, the Prime Minister; Mr. Kishi, former Prime Minister; Mr. Yoshida, another former Prime Minister who is the Churchill of Japan; the Chairman of the Joint Chiefs of Staff, with six of his generals and admirals; thirty of the top financial and business leaders, called together by the Governor of the Bank of Japan; and the Speaker of the House of Representatives.

Mr. Yoshida, the elder statesman, said to me, "Moral Re-Armament must answer the violence coming out of Red China." Prime Minister Sato is keenly interested in this conference, and the part which 100 young Japanese will play when they fly here.

The last Japanese youth delegation to Mackinac impacted their country so powerfully on their return that Prime Minister Kishi said after the 1960 riots, "Were it not for the men trained in MRA, Japan today would be behind the Bamboo Curtain."

Rajmohan Gandhi, grandson of the Mahatma, writes he is sending a force of young Indians to work with you for a year in America.

There are three distinguished young leaders of Latin America here today—Alberto Kowarick, Esteban Daranyi and Omar Ibargoyen—from Brazil, Peru and Uruguay. They have just visited Presidents Castelo Branco of Brazil and Belaunde-Terry of Peru. Dr. Priale, Speaker of the Peruvian Senate, hopes to come here. A large delegation of Latin American students is also expected.

Dr. William Close has just returned from Africa. Among the statesmen he saw were Prime Ministers Kenyatta of Kenya and Tshombe of the Congo, and Ahmed El Mahdi, dynamic young leader of the Sudan. All these men are grateful for what MRA has done to give their nations a basis for freedom.

You, as young Americans, have a chance at Mackinac this summer that no Americans have ever had. You have a chance to build the future of the world by planning with these men for forces of young Americans in turn to move out of this conference into Latin America, into Asia, into Europe, into Africa.

Masahide Shibusawa of the Japanese industrial family, for example, is calling for a world conference of youth leaders in Japan. He expects 100 young Americans to move with him from the conference throughout Asia. I hope you will go.

I hope you will give to South Vietnam what the late President Diem asked for—"a massive saturation of the ideology of Moral

Re-Armament." He said, "We are grateful for America's military and economic aid and for your sons who are giving their blood here. Without it we would be Communist. But what we must have is an idea that can answer the division, corruption and moral breakdown among our people on which Communism is feeding and advancing."

Conrad Hunte, the great West Indies cricketer, talked to me yesterday. He asked for 100 young Americans to go with him to British Guiana and the Caribbean. We must plan that here.

I give a warning to the American Indian. The three Latin American spokesmen here have their eye on you. They want you to bring your convictions and your pageant and go through the Andes mountain region from Venezuela to the Argentine and answer the bid of Castro and Red China to make the Andes the Sierra Maestra of Latin America. You know that the Red Chinese broadcast twice a week in Quechua to the Indian people out there.

To make it practical, how does freedom's revolution start? This is how it started with me. I came to Mackinac in 1946. I was still on terminal leave from the Navy, having just navigated my PC boat from the Philippines to Hawaii to Portland, Oregon.

There was a young major here who had kept Patton's Redball Highway moving across Germany. He had been here longer than the rest of us. I said to him one day, "What is this idea that people are living here?" He said, "It is very simple—absolute moral standards and a commitment to revolutionize the world."

"Very simple!" I exploded. "What do you mean, absolute moral standards?" He said, "Honesty, purity, unselfishness and love. Very simple."

I said, "That would be absolute lunacy for a Naval officer. You can't achieve that."

"Look, Belk," he said, "you have just told me you navigated your boat from the Philippines to America. There was a fixed point in the sky called the North Star. If you didn't navigate by that every day, where would you have got to?"

It suddenly flashed through my mind that for five days it had been cloudy. I couldn't see the North Star. I missed Pearl Harbor by 500 miles. So I took a new tack, and said, "What do you mean by absolute purity?" He looked me up and down and replied, "Just about the opposite of what you are living now." I got mad. He said, "Don't get angry. Try it. Experiment with it. You may find the biggest thing in your life. If you don't, you haven't lost anything. You can always go back to the mess you've been in."

16

I decided to try. I listened by myself. The thought came to me, "Everything that has 'U.S. Navy' on the back of it does not belong to J. B. Belk. Return it to Uncle Sam."

Not a very important step, but the first step on a new journey. It is getting out of reverse into forward gear. If we all take a first step here today, America will take a big first step tomorrow.

A God who is practical and straight enough to tell an ex-Navy man to return stolen gear to Uncle Sam would have a lot to say about straightening out the mess in Vietnam and Santo Domingo. People who say God is old-fashioned haven't done much listening to Him lately. God is racing at mustang speed. Most of us don't move fast enough to catch his forward passes. So we miss the fascination of His ideas for the future of the world.

That future is up to young America. You could still do what is needed for the world. You have the energy, the dynamic, the power and the stamina to do it, *if* you decide to be totally involved and committed.

But be assured of one point. Your generation is being planned for every day and every night on a world scale. The plan is clear, whether you see it or not. You are going to be animalized, Communized or atomized.

"Animalized" means going back to the jungle of the "new morality"—anything goes as long as it's done with "love."

"Communized" is a further stage when man the animal is disciplined as in a zoo. In the *New York Times* last week I read a report from Red China, "A tremendous campaign is under way to train a new and tough breed of revolutionary." The writer described them as "working in the communes until they drop with exhaustion, and then rising again and resuming work . . . animal joy is subdued, frivolity is frowned on, sex is sublimated."

"Atomized" is what Mao Tse-tung meant when he said he is prepared to sacrifice 300 million lives in an atomic war to win the world to Communism. Some Americans advocate dropping the bomb now, before China has the means to deliver it.

These courses all spell insanity. But there is a sane alternative for the world. Man can be modernized.

A modernized man is a man whose heart belongs to the whole world because it has been freed of hate, fear and greed. He has a passion for the whole world because his heart is pure. And his commitment is never to abate until every nation is governed by men governed by God.

17

RICHARD D. WAILES, *a Yale graduate in Industrial Engineering, captained the Varsity crew in 1958. He won three Gold Medals for the United States in the 1956 and 1960 Olympics and the 1959 Pan American Games and has been elected three times to the Helms Hall of Fame. With his Olympic colleague, John Sayre, whose address appears later in this volume, he went to Japan last year as part of the 1964 Olympic Team Administration. Afterwards both men were invited by the Japanese Athletic Association to set up, between now and 1970, a training program in character and fitness for two million Japanese youth. Wailes draws from his experience with Soviet and other Iron Curtain athletes the conclusion that it is as important to the cause of free democracy to win men as it is to win medals. He was Co-Director with Sayre of this year's Mackinac Island Demonstration. Mr. Wailes is 29, married and has two children.*

2

GOLD MEDALS AND RED RUSSIANS

by

Richard Wailes

WE WERE ASKED by the United States Olympic Committee to give special training to our team in Los Angeles last year before they left for Tokyo.

We spoke to every coach, trainer and athlete, men and women. We outlined for them, much as we are doing for you here, what young Americans can do in the modern world, what they are meant to do, and what is the challenge that faces this generation. We told them we are meant to be the most dynamic, far-seeing, fast-moving youth in the world today.

Our Olympic Team responded enthusiastically. Most of them said, "Why hasn't somebody told us all this sooner. Now let's go and do it."

They were in Tokyo four weeks. Three days after their arrival the Japanese press was already commenting on the new spirit and discipline of this year's American Olympic athletes.

Through the Japanese Athletic Association and their interest in Moral Re-Armament we had the chance of meeting much of the leadership of Japan, including the present Prime Minister, Mr. Sato, the former Prime Minister, Mr. Kishi, and the Speaker of the Japanese Diet or Parliament, Mr. Funada. All of these men spoke of the new spirit and behavior of the Americans, and how grateful they were for it, because it made easier their job of building friendship between our two nations.

We also had an opportunity to meet men and women from many of the nations competing in the Games. We were staying in a Japanese home. Several evenings we spent with the Russian Olympic Team. They are trained in every sense of the word. Their athletes not only win Gold Medals, but they win men and nations for their idea.

One day there was a cocktail party for all the previous winners of Gold, Silver and Bronze Medals. John Sayre was speaking. He let fly with tremendous conviction at this crowd, and the Russians, sensing that we were trying to get an idea across, quickly surrounded us at the end.

One of them, a man with an English-sounding accent, started talking with me, and I asked him where he had learned his English. He said he was the team translator, trained at Harvard. Being a Yale man myself we had an interesting dialogue. He was fascinated by the training we had given the American team, and we invited him to dinner. He came.

We sat in a friend's lovely Japanese home and had a sukiyaki meal. Those of you who have not had sukiyaki have a treat in store. The Harvard-trained translator had brought two of his Soviet friends. One he introduced as the team doctor—a huge man with a bear-like grip who was also the Team Commissar, responsible for keeping his athletes on their toes ideologically. The other was Robert Chavlakadze who won a Gold Medal in the High Jump in 1960.

We had hardly got started on the sukiyaki before the doctor started on us. "As young Americans," he demanded, "what is your aim in the modern world?" He tried to blow us right off our chairs.

We blew right back. "Our aim in the modern world," we replied, "is to equip a hundred million young Americans with an aim and purpose adequate to cure what is wrong not only in our own country but right across the earth."

This brought the Russian up short. He had never met young Americans so certain of what they wanted to give their lives to.

He said, "What are you doing with the youth of your country?" We told him what had happened last summer to 2,500 young Americans at the Conference for Tomorrow's America.

He was fascinated. He said, "What are your goals for the future?" We told him about plans to train 10,000 more young Americans this summer. "Ten thousand," he exclaimed. "That's fine, but that's just a drop in the bucket to what you need to do in your country." He had lived two years in the United States and knew this land well.

He continued, "What are some of the things you are trying to cure in America?" We spoke of the divisions in American life—the race, class, and family disunity, and how one out of every three new marriages ends in divorce.

Finally the Russian sprang to his feet. "How in the devil," he shot at us, "can you Americans expect to raise your kids right with all the sex and violence that comes over your television?" He said, "Television should be used to explain the world and to show men how to live in it."

I didn't agree of course with the ideas he would want to pump over our television, but his views of what television should be used for were interesting, and his estimate of the negative features of American television programs was also interesting.

I replied, "It is one thing to protest. Many Americans do protest. But it is another thing to try to create the right plays and films that can go out over television and radio and bring a new spirit to the whole of humanity." I continued, "You would be interested to know that those 2,500 young Americans last summer created a dozen new films that are doing that job."

"Can I see one?" he asked. "Just step into the back room," I replied. We had set it up before dinner, thinking he would ask.

This film showed some of you young Americans with a certain discipline, pace and passion, and an aim for your lives. He was amazed because, he said, he had so seldom seen Americans who lived for anything except sex, comfort and success.

At the end of the film he turned to us. "You didn't mention Russian youth in that picture. What part do we play in your revolution?"

We told him they could play a very great part. We reminded him that Russia was training her young men and women to think for the world, and before you can get young Americans to do the same, you have to cut through vast layers of selfishness and petty thinking. We told him—what he already knew—that the concern of most Americans was for their own plans and interests, and seldom for the world. I said, "If you Russians have the guts to change where you need to, you could take a new spirit to the whole world as your next step."

He was shaken. "How," he asked, "did Americans like you ever get interested in a revolution like this?"

We told him about meeting Soviet athletes in years past—men and women of our generation who at that time had far more discipline and passion in their lives than ourselves because they had

21

a bigger aim. We told him we had realized then that you could never answer that type of passion and commitment with mere anti-Communism. We reminded him that much of the world has been anti-American during the last ten or fifteen years, but it has not yet changed America. I said, "You need an idea that is big enough for every class, color and creed in the world today."

He said, "How does your revolution begin?" We told him about Moral Re-Armament, and added some of our best stories.

First I told about my income tax—how as an engineer at the Boeing Airplane Company I had been cheating the United States Government on my tax returns, and how when I went to make amends to the Income Tax Bureau, the official looked at me in dismay and protested, "You have just unbalanced my accounts!" The Russians roared.

Then I told how, when I was at Yale, I happened to be Captain of the Crew, President of the University Athletic Association, Deacon in the Church, and member of a Secret Society. But nobody knew that there were a dozen stores around New Haven that, unknown to them, supplied me regularly with books, records, clothing, and other items I contrived not to pay for. I told the Russians how I had written those stores and paid them back for everything I owed. I mentioned the replies I got from these firms—amazing replies—and how it moved them all forward.

Then I told what had happened in my own family when I was honest with my wife. Some of you have met my wife here, and if you talk with her she will back me up.

Suddenly the Russian high jumper—a man my age with two small children like me—began to shift in his chair. He said, "Getting honest with your wife—that really would be difficult." Then he was very silent. The others stared at us or looked at the ceiling. Finally one of them said, "You men are real revolutionaries. You demand of yourself the type of change you demand of the other man, the other class, the other race and the other country. Will you come and help us with our Soviet youth?"

A few nights later we were at an Embassy party, and through one of our own diplomats met the Naval Attaché of the Soviet Embassy, Admiral Nikolai Sobolev. He asked us what we were doing. We told him we worked with the world program of Moral Re-Armament. "Ah, yes," he said, "What were you doing at that youth conference last year?" He was Soviet Chief of Intelligence in Japan and knew our work.

When we finished answering his questions this Soviet Admiral commented, "It is unbelievable for me to meet young Americans like you. You know where you are going and where you want to take the world. I will call you modern Columbuses who chart a new course on an untried sea."

I tell you these stories of my Russian friends because I believe every one of you here tonight is meant to be equipped with these skills necessary to capture millions behind the Iron and Bamboo Curtains with an idea, a passion, and a plan far bigger than anything Communism has yet offered the world.

It is not going to be done by talk, by demonstrating in the streets or squatting on the sidewalks. It is going to be done by a revolutionary commitment of the hearts, minds and wills of young America—a commitment big enough to include every man, woman and child on the face of the earth. It is going to be done through a discipline and passion that can out-match any Fascist or Communist, and build a society that works.

RAJMOHAN GANDHI, *30, is a grandson of two of India's greatest leaders—Mahatma Gandhi, the revered father of Independence, and Chakravarti Rajagopalachari, first Indian Governor General. Widely regarded as spokesman for India's restless youth, he believes that given a global objective, and a resurgence of patriotism and self-sacrifice, India in cooperation with Japan can supplant Communist China as the pace-setter of Asia. Two years ago his 4,500-mile "March on Wheels" from Kerala to New Delhi dramatized these convictions. Gandhi, who has travelled and lectured extensively in the United States, Europe and Latin America, recently completed a speaking tour of Brazilian Universities. He is Editor-in-Chief of the national weekly* Himmat.

3

PLAN FOR CHINA

by

Rajmohan Gandhi

I WAS THINKING today of this mighty land America and of my own country.

I am proud to be an Indian and glad I was born that way.

I was also thinking what my feelings might be had I been born an American. If I had been born an American Indian, that would have been surely wonderful. If I had been born in a Negro family or in a white family, I'd be tremendously proud.

I would be thankful to the Almighty for making me a citizen of this land, for belonging to a nation that opens its doors to all races, to men of different backgrounds and different faiths. I'd be grateful, too, to belong to a nation that sent its soldiers to give their blood to save other nations when this country's own freedom was not immediately threatened.

I would also be grateful to belong to a nation that with unparalleled, unexampled generosity gave faith and food to nations starving and in famine throughout the world. I would be grateful to God for making me a member of a society that for the first time in history took on a responsibility for the peace, security and liberty of the entire world.

Then I would be puzzled, too, to see why, having done so much, there was considerable dislike, anger, hate towards my nation in the world. I would learn after meeting Moral Re-Armament that the reason was lack of an ideology, the lack of a revolutionary purpose and goal which is the real desire and need of the Asian, the African, the European. I would soon understand that with a common purpose· of that kind, benefiting all men everywhere and designed to transform society, my country would then meet with a

25

response from men and women of all races and nations.

I would begin to wonder, however, why before such abundant evidence of the power of this revolutionary aim, my government and the influential people of my country were not fighting for it and giving it to nation after nation. I would surely try and find out.

I imagine I would be quite angry that at this late hour, with the evidence that Moral Re-Armament could shift history, newspapers, television stations, movie makers and magazine proprietors were not giving this proven concept to the entire world.

A few weeks ago an important document was published in Moscow. It analyzes the successes and failures of Communism so far and outlines what Communists want to attain in the future. It also looks at the non-Communist world. It reaches one important conclusion:

"The nature of an economy can be changed within a relatively short period of time," the document states, "but it takes much longer to change man's character and morality. Lenin, the founder of the Soviet state, was well aware of the difficulty and long duration of this process, but he had no doubt whatsoever that a new man could be developed under socialism. It was possible, but it called for tremendous effort.

"Even now the cultivation of a spirit of friendship and comradeship among the nations remains a major problem for socialist society. It is particularly important during the transition from socialism to Communism. Certain things are incompatible with Communism—first among them are the twins of individualism and self-interest. In socialist society, too, there are hard-hearted, selfish people who put money and their own purposes above all."

This to me is an extremely interesting statement. There was a time not so long ago when people used to say, "Changing human nature is fine, but the real task is to change society." I believe we need change in both. We need strong laws to change society. And we need a revolutionary change in the nature of man so that he has an entirely new aim, and his exploitation of his fellowman can truly end.

The Communists now say that changing society is easy, passing laws is easy, liquidating people is easy. But changing the nature of man is very tough. They admit that they have not yet done it.

Khrushchev used to admit that. His admissions became more and more frequent in the last few months of his regime. Then he was deposed. Those who knew Khrushchev say that in those months

26

he was coming very close to an appreciation and understanding of Moral Re-Armament. Now the new regime in Moscow admits it officially. Furthermore, they have examined Moral Re-Armament and conclude that the only force in the non-Communist world trying to change both society and human nature is Moral Re-Armament.

I want now to speak about Vietnam. A few days ago a British politician named Patrick Gordon Walker came to America. He would have been Foreign Secretary in the Labor Cabinet but was twice defeated at the polls. He proposes for Vietnam a solution rather like this: He says that the Vietnamese are not particularly fond of the Chinese. So the best possible thing in the circumstances, he claims, is to encourage what is called a Tito-style regime in Vietnam. The idea is that you have a Communist regime that rules the whole country, but it is supposed to be independent of Peking's control—a nationalist-Communist regime.

I read an editorial in the "New York Times" welcoming this proposal.

Let me take this chance to say that men and women who want liberty in Asia will not accept this solution. They are not particularly keen that non-Asian nations in other parts of the world should impose a Communist regime, call it Tito-style if you want, on an Asian nation like Vietnam. We don't want it. The people of Vietnam don't want it.

There is one other point. It is extraordinary to me that a man like Mr. Gordon Walker, who I imagine is very sincere and intelligent, should bring his mind to bear on a problem like Vietnam without thinking through the next step to follow. Supposing you have a Tito-style Communist regime in Vietnam—though I think it is impossible to prove that it will be independent of Peking—what happens to neighboring nations?

What happens to Thailand? Marshal Chen Yi, the Chinese Foreign Minister, spoke recently about soon "starting another Vietnam in Thailand." These are his openly proclaimed threats or promises, whichever way you look at it.

If you have a Tito-style Communist regime in Vietnam, there will soon be a clamor for the same kind of regime in Thailand. The next step is a Tito-style Communist regime in Malaysia, then the Philippines, then Pakistan, then Ceylon—finally in India. And so on until you recommend Tito-style Communist regimes for every country in Asia and Africa.

I wonder how Mr. Gordon Walker would feel about a Tito-style Communist regime, say, in Ireland. I don't imagine he would feel too comfortable about it.

Vietnam is the occasion, the point of contact for the great struggle between the Communist and non-Communist world. It could have been any other part of the world that symbolized this struggle. Today it happens to be Vietnam.

I believe a solution can still come to Vietnam, and that America still holds the key. But it will require a radical revolutionary change in the attitude of both our countries. The United States has got to learn that you cannot win an ideological war without an ideology. It is a point that simply must be understood if there is to be any chance of a genuine solution out there.

A corollary of this is the attitude toward the late President Diem who was killed. Diem wanted a moral ideology for Vietnam. He was not a perfect man. Neither were his relatives. But Diem did want, as he told me, "to saturate the country with Moral Re-Armament." He understood the heart of the matter—that the people of Vietnam wanted a revolution superior to the Communist revolution.

Vietnam's problems are the same as the problems of all Asia and Africa. They need economic progress. They need to learn to work hard, honestly and unitedly. They need a stable, incorruptible leadership. They need a fearless populace, who will not be terrorized by the Viet Cong or lured by the blandishments of the Communists. They need some solution for the divisions between Buddhists and Catholics. They need an ideology which can unite all the different tribes, castes, racial groups inside that country.

Diem felt Moral Re-Armament could bring the unity, incorruptibility and fearlessness before Communist threats and pressures, that the country needed. For various reasons he was stopped. Before he could proceed with his program, his regime was destroyed.

Now I understand that "girlie" shows have been suggested to raise the morale of the Vietnamese. If anyone thinks that such things are going to give these people an idea of liberty, inspire them to fight more courageously, and win them over to the free world, I can assure him he is wrong. These shows will only weaken any moral fiber left in Vietnam, and directly and indirectly increase Communist influence. The free world must understand that freedom has a straightforward, moral basis; that immorality is a definite, unfailing precursor of tyranny.

I can assure you, as an Asian, that no amount of military strength, much as we need and appreciate it, can in itself make up for ideological weakness. For instance, some people say America should bomb more and somehow win the battle, but haven't a plan of what to do after the battle is won. Others say we must go to the conference table and negotiate, but haven't the slightest idea what to do when we meet the Vietcong, the North Vietnamese, or the Chinese face to face. They have no idea how our opponents can be influenced and changed.

Here again I believe the key to the dilemma is in America's hand. If you have Moral Re-Armament in Vietnam, if your troops and State Department officials are MRA-trained, if you have unity within your country and unity with your friends and allies, it is possible to meet and change Communists.

Many people ask me about the Peace Corps. Now many of the Peace Corps men and women are great idealists who really want to do something for the world. But frankly it isn't enough today to go and teach nations in Asia and Africa a language, scientific or political techniques, or methods of sanitation, important though these are. What is absolutely essential is to produce men and women in those nations who can lead their people, who will be dependable, who will be reliable, whose work can be trusted, who will work hard, who will be solid leaders. You can't actually do a job in those nations if you don't know how to deal with the character of men; and that technique, that revolutionary skill the Peace Corps does not teach. I feel that the great idealism of these men and women should be used, that they should be solidly, properly trained in Moral Re-Armament, and when that happens I believe the Peace Corps will achieve its purposes.

You will know how to go about it, but I think what really ought to be achieved is to transform the Peace Corps into an ideological corps, or a new world corps if you like—give it any name you want —but let its aim be far more than just peace. Let its aim be to create a new world, to modernize man and his society, to give a new ideology to the world. Let's make it a full, complete, relevant force dealing with the basic problems of the modern world. I see no reason why President Johnson shouldn't require the Peace Corps, and all other U.S. officials serving abroad, to be ideologically trained before they're sent out.

If we seized the ideological offensive with both hands, we could have a hundred-to-one superiority over China, or Russia, and the respect of the entire non-Communist world.

Look at the Asian scene again. Vietnam is one country. You also have Thailand, Taiwan, the Philippines, Malaysia, Indonesia, Ceylon, Pakistan, India, Japan, Korea, Hong Kong.

The secret of success in South-east Asia lies in capturing these other nations for Moral Re-Armament. Such a major offensive would produce disarray in Chinese ranks. It would produce instability and insecurity inside China and North Vietnam, but unity inside Saigon and South Vietnam. If only the non-Communist world understood this simple point.

Indonesia can be won. There are thousands of Indonesian students in Australia, Japan and the Philippines. Can we not give them Moral Re-Armament and send them back? One of the major aims of the free world in Asia should be to invade Indonesia ideologically. If you did that you would produce a dividing line in Indonesia —of the right kind. You would win that country.

Suppose in Malaysia and Singapore you succeeded in welding Malays, Chinese and Indians into a strong, stable nation, creating there the launching pad for a militant moral ideology reaching into Rangoon, Jakarta, Hanoi and the whole of South-East Asia? Suppose you did that also in Thailand, before Chen Yi starts his activities? Suppose you did the same in Taiwan, and in Japan? Suppose Japan, as she is well on the road to doing, should become as committed to Moral Re-Armament as China is to Communism? The news would reach Peking instantly and the people of China would take hope.

Frankly, China is far more important than Vietnam. We are straining every nerve to resolve Vietnam, but we need to plan at the same time how to change China. With the Asian nations around China committed to Moral Re-Armament, the day will come when we can challenge the Chinese Government and people to examine and accept this greater ideology.

To bring these things about, we shall need large sums of money. We shall need planes, carrying large forces of young Americans, South Americans and Europeans to Asian lands. We shall need plays, and we shall need machines.

We shall also need a few things far more important than that— brave men and women, prepared to take not just a year or two, but perhaps five or ten, or their whole life, to live in and try to change those lands. We shall need men and women prepared to stand discomfort and strange food. You will have to risk disease and separation from loved ones.

You will need to learn the languages of those nations. That will take hard work. You will need to learn to teach techniques of agriculture, industry, sanitation and medicine. Above all you will need to learn the secret that has so far eluded both Communist and non-Communist nations—the secret of modernizing man, of changing the character of men you meet, of making them strong, fearless and incorruptible.

Many take it for granted that China and Russia will stay Communist. I don't. I believe Communism in China and Russia can be superseded provided we of the non-Communist world, while matching them in the military field, resolve to more than match them in the decisive field of ideology. If Americans will lead us in this task, they will do for the world what Washington and Lincoln once did for the American Republic, and they will find all patriotic, freedom-loving Asians at their side.

MORRIS MARTIN, M.A., D. PHIL. (Oxon) *graduate of Wadham College, Oxford, had a brilliant academic career as Harmsworth Senior Student of Merton College and youngest Doctor of Philosophy of his time. For twenty-three years he travelled the world as personal secretary to Dr. Frank N. D. Buchman, initiator of Moral Re-Armament, and is currently at work on his biography. He was also a close colleague of Buchman's successor, the late Peter Howard, whom he first met on the football field at Oxford when they were undergraduates. Dr. Martin, 55, is married and lives in Rome.*

4

THREE-STAGE ROCKET
TO REVOLUTION

by

Morris Martin

Today I am going to tell you briefly about Frank Buchman,
starting with an outline picture of his whole life. He was like a
three-stage rocket. You know how a rocket goes up—first stage,
second stage, third stage and then it is in orbit.

The first stage of Frank Buchman's life was powered by a
passionate concern about poverty, about homelessness, and about
the state of America at the turn of the century. He poured his life
into doing something about those problems, and the passion to help
people was the motive power of his life at that first stage.

But when the rocket reaches a certain point, that second stage
has to cut in. If it doesn't, the rocket comes down. A lot of people
in their lives reach a ceiling; they never go above it because they
are only concerned to carry through their own plans. That was the
first stage of Frank Buchman's life. He wanted to carry through
his own plan: a good plan, but limited to what he could do.

Buchman saw why he reached this ceiling. It was because in
dealing with the social problem he did not deal fundamentally with
people, therefore difficult people remained difficult. He had to find
a power to carry him through to the next stage.

The second stage of his rocket was the changing of individual
men to give them new motives so as to build a new world. It had
to begin with a change in himself. Then he could change others
and launch them out in their families, homes and colleges, into
trade unions, management, the affairs of nations, the places where
battles had to be fought. That was the next stage of his life.

Then came the final stage, the third stage of the rocket, when
Buchman challenged the whole world with its need for God-control.

When a missile is in orbit, it does not feel the pull of earth any more. It is free. His conception was that men should be free to be controlled by God, free of the pull of race and class, of hate, greed and fear. He didn't want to see a world controlled by Moscow, or by Peking. He didn't want to see a world controlled only by Washington. He wanted to see a world actually controlled by God. His last words were: "I want to see the world governed by men governed by God. Why not let God run the whole world?"

That is a quick sketch of the three great motive powers of his life. The passion to change the world and the society in which people live; the realization this could not be done unless men changed, which led him to commit his life to changing men in order to change the world; and finally the challenge to the whole world, every nation, every man to accept the control of God's Will. That is the simple picture of his life.

Frank Buchman was born in 1878 at Pennsburg, Pennsylvania. His family came to America from Switzerland in 1740, before the Revolution. He had some great qualities in his heritage. One of the family traditions was to be a fighter. A second was a strong sense of right and wrong.

One ancestor fought with George Washington. Another enlisted on the side of Abraham Lincoln, the very day Lincoln first called for volunteers. If you go to Anoka, Minnesota, you will find there a plaque stating the fact. Frank Buchman was proud that his family were fighters, because he felt that it was the job of every man in every way to fight for what is right.

He started to work in the Philadelphia slums. He founded the first hospice, where young men coming in from the country to look for jobs could live, instead of just drifting around town and finally going back to the country disillusioned. It had great success. He gave good food, cheap lodging, endless personal care, but basic problems remained unchanged. He learned here that human nature had to be dealt with, or there would be no permanent change in society.

He was working terribly hard and finally realized that the basic fault was in him; he said, "I have been asking God to help me do what I wanted, and have hated anybody who tried to stop me." The great change in his life came when he said, "Now I am going to ask God to tell me what He wants me to do, and I will obey Him without question." He learnt that when God's Will crossed his and he chose God's Will, a new power came into his life.

34

This opened the second stage of his career and made him a revolutionary. It is true throughout history that the moment a man gets hitched to something bigger than his own will, he becomes a revolutionary force.

He began to work out his revolutionary ideas on the changing of men at Penn State College (now University), which he always called his laboratory, the place where for seven years he worked out his experiment. His principle was, "Two or three walking miracles will dynamite any college."

The *Yale Magazine* of that era mentioned Buchman's work as the most outstanding thing happening in the universities of America. One professor wrote, "The work that this man is doing is phenomenal, and I use that word with the full sense of its meaning."

In 1915, though urged to stay, he felt his work at Penn State was done and he went to Asia. The countries he came to know first outside America were India, China, Korea and Japan, and for the next four years he spent most of his time in them. This brought him in touch with a wholly different world, where he found the West represented by businessmen and missionaries. He found that businessmen were very busy at their business, and missionaries were very busy doing exactly what he had been doing back in Philadelphia, working very hard, very unselfishly, but largely ineffectively.

Buchman said, "It is not our job to rush around trying to answer all the problems of these countries. Our job is to change men—to relate the people of these countries to the answering of their own problems. Our job is to fit them to take on their nations."

In Japan he first met Viscount Shibusawa, a great-grandfather of Masahide Shibusawa who is here today, one of the men who brought the industrial age to Japan. He also knew Dr. Sun Yat-sen, Father of the Chinese Revolution of 1911, and Mahatma Gandhi, grandfather of Rajmohan Gandhi who spoke here recently.

Back in America after the first world war, he enlisted a force of youth to work with him. He began to make links between the universities of America and the universities of Europe. He came to Oxford University in England, and was invited one night to attend a philosophical discussion. Usually in Oxford we meet and discuss at great length and decide very little. Frank Buchman was finally invited to speak. One man in the room, who that day decided he was going to stick with Buchman for life, recalled the event: "The moment he began talking the atmosphere changed. He picked up some thread in the discussion and used it to weave his pattern.

He began to tell of changed lives, changes in men so like ourselves that interest was riveted at once. We were forced to draw our own conclusions."

Then came the Thirties when the world launched into its great struggles with Communism and Fascism. Battles were going on in the streets of many European capitals. Buchman believed that the democracies should demonstrate a revolutionary faith big enough to neutralize the Nazis and change Hitler's course. But the politicians wanted appeasement, and Hitler wanted war. War came.

At that point Frank Buchman moved into the third stage of his life, the launching of Moral Re-Armament as a force that would strengthen democracy in the face of Nazism, create a revolution powerful enough to supersede Communism, and rebuild the world after the fighting was over.

During the war a summary of his aims in America was described by the War Department as "the best statement of this nation's philosophy of national defense that has yet been written." And the Selective Service System referred to MRA as "an essential element" of our national strength.

While the men he trained were fighting and dying on most of the world's battlefields, Buchman constantly said, "We must think beyond winning the war. We must prepare men who will solve the problems of peace."

Intensely realistic about Nazism—so much so that the Gestapo condemned MRA and liquidated its men—Buchman was equally realistic about Communism. Quick to realize that mere anti-Communism will never bring an answer, he nevertheless knew that in a totalitarian age free men must always be ready to defend freedom with arms.

He also knew that Communism's success was in large part due to its power as an ideology, and that ultimately it could only be met and turned by a greater ideology. Among his memorable wartime sayings was, "A true patriot must have an idea in his head and a passion in his heart, as well as a gun in his hand."

After the war there was a widespread feeling in Europe that something new had to come, and Chancellor Adenauer of Germany, Foreign Minister Robert Schuman of France, and Prime Minister de Gasperi of Italy began to work to this end. It was through Buchman that Schuman and Adenauer met; his inspiration was behind the Schuman Plan, the merger of the Coal and Steel industries of France and Germany, and the growth of a united Europe.

It was the same story in many parts of the world. In North Africa they will tell you today that Tunisia was saved from a war like that in Algeria because of the understanding men of Moral Re-Armament created between Tunisia and France. There was a similar development in Morocco. In Nigeria, some of the first steps towards independence were due to Moral Re-Armament. Kenya largely owes its present stability to the change MRA brought to former leaders of Mau Mau.

Faced by the troubles in Little Rock and the Southern States, Frank Buchman invited Africans to America because, he said, the black American would not listen to the white American, the white American would not listen to the black American, but they both would listen to the African. They played "Freedom," the first all-African play and color feature film, in those cities and were able to meet and talk with everybody, white and Negro. Of Moral Re-Armament's part in solving the crisis in Little Rock, a year's end radio network round-up stated it was "possibly the most significant news of the year which could mark the end of a hundred years' civil war in the United States."

Buchman's knowledge of the world gave him a sense of generalship. The guidance of God gave him a daily strategy. Most significant internationally was the fact that he was an American. He was an American at a crucial time in history, giving a great idea to the world. America has given immense amounts of money—the Marshall Plan is one of the greatest acts of generosity on record—and she has received a great deal of criticism in return. That happens when you only give things, unless with the things you give an idea—a reason why you are doing it. Buchman gave the world an idea for which America and all the nations could work together.

He died four years ago, in August 1961. But his challenge and his vision had been big enough to capture men like Peter Howard, and he left behind a growing world force who fight today on every continent for the government of God which is the aim of Moral Re-Armament.

Today there is an atmosphere of permissiveness, humanism and rejection of authority, which contrasts totally with the world of Frank Buchman's youth, and with the traditional concepts of religion, education and parental upbringing which have formed society in the past.

Buchman challenged this prevailing atmosphere of our age. He built upon people, following the thread of moral need in those he met. He touched their deepest longings, turned them towards a God in whom at first they might not believe, armed them with the simple weapons of four absolute moral standards of a Christ of whom they might never have heard, and helped their belief in the direction of God to grow, and with it the desire to pass on to others what they had learned.

He lived out fully what he expected of others. "Some of you are faithful but you haven't the fire of the revolutionary," he would say. "The person who is not a whole-hogger is easily swamped. Individual rebirth must issue in national rebirth." He often quoted, "No heart is pure that is not also passionate." "Some of you never speak with passion," he said. "If there is any place where you feel I don't give myself fully, just tell me. My job is to be a bomb. I must be myself."

The early morning hours were the time when he drew from the well of God's truth. "Four a.m.," he wrote in 1940, "for more than thirty years this hour has been the best of the twenty-four— the sanest, cleanest, calmest. It was a great discipline at the beginning. I like the morning because the noise of the day has not come; the world has not begun to hum; it's quiet. It is then, with one's Bible and the Holy Spirit as the guide, that one gets direction for superhuman tasks. You don't get very far if you chuck the Bible overboard. You don't get a Lincoln without a Bible."

This was the essence of Frank Buchman, a spirit rooted in simple, universal, timeless truths of God and man, who neither looked too good nor talked too wise, a great friend, a tireless fighter for the statesman and the ordinary man to change, whose final challenge, "Why not let God run the whole world?", carried with it the promise, "The future belongs to the men who give all."

What are the lessons of Frank Buchman's life?

He spoke of having seen in his lifetime the retreat of faith, the advance of materialism and the counter-attack of Moral Re-Armament across the world. His life was devoted to creating and shaping that counter-attack. His genius was to express it in terms of a moral battle that everyone understands and everyone, if he chooses, can fight.

A morally indecisive nation breeds at best fair-weather patriots. Frank Buchman linked the battle for man's character with a nation's survival. What responsible historians recognize—that sexual anarchy breeds drab imagination, decadent art and self-centered living that rejects greatness in personal or national life—was for him a tested fact of spiritual experience, only to be answered on that level.

A man is what he believes, a nation is what it aims at, a civilization stands or falls by its standards and its purposes.

True patriotism is to give a nation the simple purpose of obeying God's will. No materialist faith can do this. The most dedicated Communist must divide the world in uniting his section of it. The most selfless nationalist must split continents while giving all for his nation. The true patriot, said Frank Buchman, gives his life to bring his nation and its leaders under God's control.

So for Frank Buchman the final struggle was for men to obey God. He had no patience with bishops who canonized their cleverness, nor scientists who worshipped their brains, nor protesters who never moved to cure anyone or anything. For him the road to certainty was by experience, honest experiment and obedience.

He longed for his own land, America, to be what Emerson called her, "God's last chance to make a world"—a world not in any man's image, any hero's image, but in God's. He has left that heritage to every American.

WILLIAM T. CLOSE, M.D., *of Greenwich, Connecticut comes from one of America's pioneer families. Brought up in Paris, where his father was Director of the American Hospital, he received his early education in France and England, attended St. Paul's School in Concord, N.H., and left Harvard to serve three years as an Air Force pilot in the European Theater. He received his M.D. in 1951 from Columbia College of Physicians and Surgeons and became Senior Surgical Resident at Roosevelt Hospital, New York. In 1960 Dr. Close went to the Congo during the crisis over independence, and volunteered as surgeon at the 1800-bed Congolese Hospital in Leopoldville, averaging 350 operations a month. During a year and a half he won for himself a unique position of trust and was appointed by General Mobutu Medical Director of the Congolese Army. He has travelled widely in Africa. Dr. Close, who was Medical Director of the Mackinac Demonstration, is 41 years old, married, and has a son and three daughters.*

5

AFRICA'S CHALLENGE TO WASHINGTON

by

William T. Close

Two weeks ago I was talking to one of the world's wealthiest men. He assured me that things would continue to go his way, and that for him the future held no terrors or threats. As we parted, his wife, who had been quite silent, said, "All the same, I do worry about what will happen to people like us when the revolution comes." Her husband spun around and said with considerable feeling, "Nothing is going to happen, you must stop worrying about it." The violence of his reply revealed his own real fears.

Last month I was in Guinea. The Ambassador for Guinea to Paris is a physician like me. We speak the same language. We talked frankly about Africa and the United States. He said, "I appreciate your frankness. I was in America recently. I went with good expectations but was disappointed. Certainly the United States is far in advance of other countries in technological development, but there seems to be a disparity between the development of science and the development in the character and morals of your citizens."

When I told him about our conference here last year and this year—a conference which will raise in the United States the level of moral maturity so that it matches our material maturity—he asked me to go to Guinea and tell the President about it.

The world today is divided between those who seek to preserve the status quo, because they think change will make things worse for them; and those who struggle to alter the status quo, because they are convinced that change can only be for the better. History is on the side of the changers, for even the most conservative realize that change is normal to human society.

41

Donald Tyneman of *The Economist* wrote a month ago, "Change of course is just another name for history. It goes on all the time. There are those who chase after all change everywhere . . . there are those to whom change is always unfriendly and to be resisted. The way of sense in both politics and business is a third way: it is to recognize that changes are happening anyhow, to use them and adapt them in pursuit of both interest and principle . . . to ride history with a purpose, not to be ridden or unseated by it."

Will the West ride history with a purpose, or be unseated by it?

Two major philosophies compete to influence the course of history. There are those who believe in the dignity of man—all men —and their God-given rights and freedoms. These men seek freedom from the bondage of disease, hunger and physical misery. They do not regard freedom as license to do as they please. To them free men are those who, as responsible sons of the Living God, fear no one, and aim towards total freedom from hate and fear and lust and arrogance—passions which bind men to those who exploit human nature in the interests of their ideology.

Then there are those who say that man is an animal. Beria, former Head of the Russian Secret Police, describes man in the following terms:

"Man is an animal which has been given a civilized veneer. Man is a collective animal grouped together for his own protection against the threats of his environment. Those who so group and control him must then have in their possession specialized techniques to direct the vagaries and energies of the animal man towards greater efficiency in the accomplishment of the goals of the state."

There are few places in the world where the struggle between these two philosophies is being more dramatically played out than in Africa.

Premier Chou En-lai of China has just been in Tanzania. His current tactic is to offer help with the railroad which would extend Chinese influence into Zambia's vitally important copper mines and within easy reach of the cobalt needed to build up nuclear capability. China appears to want a "yellow belt" across the center of Africa. Right now she has powerful influence in Zanzibar and Dar es Salaam on the east coast and Pointe Noire, port of the former French Congo, on the west coast. If China's sphere of influence includes Zambia, the "yellow belt" will be complete.

Chou En-lai's objective is clearly stated in a recent editorial from the *Japan Times* of Tokyo. "What Mr. Chou is trying to do is to rally the young nations of Africa against this country (the U.S.A.) and its policies. Thus, we find him saying that the 'struggles of the people of Vietnam and the Dominican Republic give strong support for the struggles of the people of the Congo (Leopoldville) and all Africa.'

"This attempt to align events in the Dominican Republic with rebel activities in the Congo is extremely significant. Mr. Chou evidently regards the rebel movement in the Dominican Republic as not only anti-American but favorable to Communist ambitions, and that it is therefore one to be linked up with the rebellion in the Congo."

I foresee violent times ahead. The Sudan enters crucial days this month. The Russians who left Nairobi went to Khartoum. The Communists who operate openly there, if defeated by legal means, are likely to launch attacks of terror and intimidation. A few days ago a judge who had passed down a decision unfavorable to the Communists had his house burnt down.

In Brazzaville, across the river from Leopoldville, there has been a massive arms build-up. In September an Algerian ship brought Chinese weapons. In October an English ship brought Chinese weapons. In January a Russian ship brought Russian weapons and a Dutch ship brought Chinese weapons. In February a Chinese ship brought more Chinese weapons. The Director of Information in Brazzaville brags, "We have enough to arm 800,000 Congolese." But the Brazzaville Congo Army has only one battalion.

In Leopoldville it will take supreme statesmanship on the part of Premier Tshombe, President Kasavubu and General Mobutu to maintain effective unity.

The basic ideological conflict in the world was expressed by Prime Minister Julius Nyerere of Tanzania in February, 1960. He said, "In the world there is a conflict between those who advocate freedom of the individual and those who champion the primacy of the state. The differences between Eastern and Western ideologies can be reduced to this conflict. The West has exaggerated the idea of freedom to the point where it becomes a social license permitting any form of self-indulgence in the name of personal liberty. The Communist world, largely as a reaction against this exaggeration, has swung to the other extreme. The individual in a Communist State is secondary to the State."

43

Looking at events around the world, something seems to be missing on the side of the so-called Western forces of freedom. Could it be that in spite of our military and economic might we have yet to learn a simple fact—namely that the key to success in the war of ideas is the human factor of winning people. Could it be that all too often the way we live, and what we live for, are in contradiction to the principles and ideals we proclaim?

Let me give you an example from my own home. A few years ago I heard one of my children talking to a visitor: "Dad used to talk to us a lot about our manners and behavior. It did not impress us until one day we noticed that he himself had become less grumpy. Then we started to listen."

For the past five years I have been intimately involved in the Congo. I have seen the struggle between those who say there is no God, and use terror and hate to make their way, and those who say there is a God, but all too often live in a way that makes many wonder if He really exists.

Following are a set of rules of conduct which have been used in the war of ideas. I list them:

1. Act in accordance with orders.
2. Do not take anything from the people.
3. Do not allow self-interest to injure public interest.
4. Talk pleasantly.
5. Tidy up when you are about to leave a place.
6. Pay for anything you damage.
7. Do not bathe in the view of women.
8. Do not take advantage of those for whom you are responsible.

These sound rules are actually orders used by the Viet Cong in Southeast Asia, and some of the rebels called Viet Congolese in the Congo. They were first drawn up by Mao Tse-tung of China.

It is common knowledge that the deportment and morals of troops fighting under the banner of anti-God are often better than those of the so-called forces of God and freedom. This is often why we Americans lose respect and confidence abroad, and are out of touch with so much of the population in areas of ideological conflict.

In a recent interview with American journalist Edgar Snow, Mao Tse-tung pointed out that "the West seems to ignore the decisive political fact that governments cut off from the masses cannot win in wars of national liberation."

Why have we been missing the boat in areas like South-east Asia and Central Africa? Because there are too few men and women who have the moral authority to fight straight on basic moral issues. These basic moral issues are the most important factors in the ideological struggle. Let me give you an example.

Not long ago an officer in the Congolese Army came to my house and said, "Doctor, you should go and talk to Colonel So-and-So. His men are losing respect for him because he fools around so much at night that his work suffers. He's a security risk and you ought to do something to help him." I asked this officer why he did not help his friend himself, but he made some lame excuse. In fact, he was horsing around at night himself and was in no position to tackle his friend.

Later I did go to see the Colonel and told him this story: "When I was a pilot in the Air Force during the war we had to land in Paris for the night. Next morning I came out to the aircraft in poor shape and my Crew Chief put his hand on my shoulder. 'Lieutenant,' he said, 'it does not go when your crew see you coming back from town in this shape and we know you must fly us during the day. You must grow up.' That shook me at the time, and when I told the Congolese Colonel the story it shook the daylights out of him. He said, 'Thank you, I get the point.'"

The forces of anti-God and tyranny are advancing in certain areas of Africa, not through their Communist dialectic or ideas, but through the corruption and impurity of some of the Western-backed leaders. Surely if the forces of anti-God use hate, fear, corruption and lust to capture people, God-fearing men should seek to cure fear and hate, and to bring an answer to corruption and lust.

Take the so-called civilized Western embassies in Leopoldville and compare them to the unsophisticated Congolese Army. I had more moral medical problems to handle in the Western embassies than in an entire Congolese battalion!

In one African country the Chief of State has an Achilles heel —women. In that same country one man representing the United States lives a life of such debauchery that he has lost the respect of African leaders and is in no position to help the Chief of State.

Some of us in the West glibly blame the Communists for the trouble in the world. That is cheap and unproductive. Their ideology is certainly wrong, and they are certainly fomenting trouble on a massive scale. But surely our task as free men and women must be to cure the causes of Communism and demonstrate in our own society a more compelling idea.

45

I would like to tell you what happened to me during the mutiny in Leopoldville. On the first day I went over to the City Hospital of 1800 beds and introduced myself to the Belgian nun in charge of the operating room. I said I would be glad to give them a hand. She welcomed this and called over her young Congolese assistant, Sam.

Sam was an operating room technician who turned out to be one of the leaders of Kasavubu's Youth Wing. He took one look at me and said, "I want you to know that the answer for this country comes over Radio Moscow twice a day." He went to every pavilion and told the patients that if they fell into the hands of the American surgeon they would be killed.

My second day at the hospital was far the worst. We had two operating rooms going. In one there was an older Belgian surgeon operating on some white people who had been mobbed. He had the Sister as his assistant. I was in the other working on some Congolese soldiers who had been shot, with Sam as my assistant. There was terror everywhere. Troops were all over the city, in and out of the hospital, and I am not the sort of surgeon who does his best work with men running around with tommy guns. But the worst element that morning was the bitterness between the two operating rooms. The Belgian doctor ran out of one of the gases used for anaesthesia but wouldn't come into my operating room for more. We ran out of catgut but none of my Congolese personnel would go next door for more. This made work almost impossible.

While I was operating on a trooper with a bullet in his thigh I turned and said to Sam, "Sam, I was thinking about you early this morning. I thought that the arrogance and superiority in some white doctors has made you bitter and I am darn sorry for it. But there are many of us giving our lives to put that right."

There was a long silence. Finally Sam said, "You are the first white doctor I've known with the guts to admit he is wrong."

During the rest of the morning I told him of places in my life where I had needed to change. At the end of a very tough day Sam went out of the room and came back with a wet towel. He got down on the floor to wipe the plaster of Paris off my shoes. I got down on the floor with him. He said, "I have got to meet some of your friends in Moral Re-Armament."

The next two weeks were hell. The Sister and Sam loathed each other. She used to give Sam hell, and Sam gave her back the same. She was white, he was black; she was Belgian, he was Congolese;

46

she was Catholic, he was Protestant; she was the boss, he was determined he was going to be. It got to the point that they wouldn't work in the same room.

One day Sam came to her and said, "Sister, I realize we cannot build this country on the basis of hate and bitterness, and I have hated you and the Belgians. I want your forgiveness and need your help to be different."

That evening the Sister called Sam to the operating room and said, "Sam, I am the one who needs to ask forgiveness. I have bitterly resented the way you have treated us whites. Also I have been afraid of you. I am the one who needs to change."

The three of us sat down and worked out a modus operandi which enabled us to do an average of 350 operations a month for a year and a half. We could never have done it if Sam and the Sister, and a proud American surgeon, had not found the grace of Almighty God to cure hate and fear and pride.

There is no other country in the world with the military, intellectual and scientific capabilities of the United States. Many countries envy our wealth but expect from us something more. In Kenya, the leader of Jomo Kenyatta's Youth Wing is a militant young African nationalist. He wears a Lumumba button and because I took care of Gizenga (Lumumba's heir) when he was in prison, we got along from the first. Not long ago he drove me to the airport at Nairobi. Waiting for the plane I asked him, "If you were speaking to American leaders, what would you ask them for your country?" He said, "I would ask them for teachers, doctors, engineers and all the people we need to help raise our standard of living." He paused, then added with passion, "But above all, we need young men and women who by the discipline and purpose in their own lives can give our youth a new direction."

I love my country enough to go anywhere to serve her and the God she professes to believe in. I want to see a new type of American—virile, clean, healthy, passionate—representing us at home and overseas. I want other nations to look at Americans and say not only, "I wish I had the know-how he has in his head and the money he has in his pocket," but also, "I wish I had the ideas he has in his heart and lives in his life."

MASAHIDE SHIBUSAWA, *business executive, is a son of former Finance Minister and Governor of the Bank of Japan, Viscount Keizo Shibusawa, and a great-grandson of Viscount Eiichi Shibusawa who in 1867 first opened his country to Western industry and science. With Saburo Chiba, Senior Adviser to the Liberal-Democratic Party, and Governor Shinji Sogo of the National Railways, he pioneered construction of the Asian Center for Moral Re-Armament at Odawara near Mt. Fuji. A friend and adviser to government leaders, Shibusawa was the first Japanese to be received by the Korean Prime Minister following the recent Japan-Korea Treaty. His new book on the ideological struggle in Asia, "Design for Revolution," is currently a best-seller in Tokyo. Mr. Shibusawa, 40, is married and has two children.*

6

A THEME FOR NATIONHOOD

by

Masahide Shibusawa

K ARL MARX said one hundred years ago, "Workers of the world unite!" The workers, at least a great many of them, united and marched with him. It generated a colossal power which changed the course of history. This morning I felt you young men and women of America can now say, "Youth of the world unite and march with us!" If you succeed in winning the new generation of the world and get them to march with you, you would have the future in your hands.

Every nation on earth today is conscious of the need for a new theme and purpose for its nationhood. Communist states are discovering that the philosophy of class war is too limited a concept, so that at the very moment they might be able to conquer the world, they find unity within their own ranks impossible. Among the free nations it becomes clearer every day that national self-interest is too small an aim to rally their peoples for the tasks ahead, and that wealth and know-how are no substitute for purpose. In Asia, with the Communist threat near at hand, we feel this deeply and you sense an almost physical hunger for a great idea.

I was in Seoul two weeks ago when the controversial treaty between Korea and Japan was signed. The Prime Minister welcomed me, saying it was significant that a representative of Moral Re-Armament was the first Japanese to be received after he signed it. I told him I came to find out how best we could together help Korea at this stage of history. He replied that our former Prime Minister Kishi had told him about MRA, that he felt it was the idea Korea most needed today, and that he would like to have an MRA Assembly in Seoul. There was a student demonstration against the treaty going on in the streets outside his office as we talked, and he especially responded to the idea of having a student conference and a new type of demonstration in the capital.

Next I met the Minister of Education. He was rather exhausted and frustrated by the street demonstrations, and when I suggested bringing a force of revolutionary youth to the city, his first reaction was, "Please, we have enough of them here already!" When he realized that MRA was a different kind of revolution, he responded warmly to Korean student leaders being invited for training at Mackinac Island, and immediately arranged for us to meet the students at the heart of the demonstrations in Seoul. These proved to be first class young men. Some had just come out of jail, others were awaiting sentence. They responded to Moral Re-Armament. Several will be on the chartered plane that is arriving at Mackinac from Japan.

The present leaders of Korea are men of action. They went through the bitter experience of the Korean War fighting shoulder to shoulder with American officers and troops. Many were educated in the military academies of the United States. They are impatient to get things done. And they have done an outstanding job for their country in the past three years. Exports have multiplied six times, from a value of $20 million three years ago to $120 million last year. This year they may well exceed $200 million—a colossal achievement. Three years ago, for instance, they had to import cement, a basic commodity, but now they have so much cement that they are exporting it.

You sense in Korea today a new vigor and hope. Businessmen are much more confident. There is no question that if the country can now be given a big idea to inspire her youth, heal her divisions and mobilize every man, woman, and child in the service of the nation, there is no limit to what she can do for Asia and the world.

Korea is staunchly anti-Communist. This is understandable because of her very bitter experience with Communism. But anti-Communism is a sterile idea. It cannot win enemies, or unite friends, and it tends to isolate a country. What Korea needs beyond her determination to keep the Communists at a distance, is an ideology that can re-direct and transform them.

I think of the war in Vietnam. I am grateful the United States is fighting there. If your country withdrew from Vietnam now, believe me the continent of Asia would be finished. This is a war that must be fought. But to stop Communism is too limited a goal. You need to give the Vietnamese and the Asians a vision more appealing and an idea more powerful than anything Communism can offer.

I believe the issue today is whether America can re-direct the heart and mind of Communist China. If America fails to do that, regardless of the results of battles or even wars here and there, America will lose in the world, and the result will be disaster for all mankind. I believe the great value of your stand in Vietnam is that it gains time in which your nation and mine can join in making Moral Re-Armament accepted on every continent as the theme and goal for humanity.

I want to invite many of you to Japan and Korea this autumn. I want to see a demonstration of youth, not to attack or divide or revolt, but to create a new climate in the world. I want these nations you visit to find three things:

1. The secret of unity. Any fool can divide the world in this age. It takes genius, courage and dedication to unite the world. We must make division out of date and unity the fashion of tomorrow.

2. An answer to poverty. The time has come for our nations to make it their prime objective to answer the poverty in Asia, Africa and Latin America. It is absolutely wrong to keep hundreds of millions of people unable to have two meals a day. We must wage an all-out war against poverty on a world scale.

3. A new theme for nationhood. National self-interest, however enlightened, is too small an aim for modern nations. We must transform and enlarge our thinking so that we live for all men everywhere instead of for one nation, one class or one race.

I want you to go to every capital in Asia and proclaim this answer. I don't lure you by pleasure or comfort. Revolution demands everything from revolutionaries. When Mahatma Gandhi set out to win the independence of India 100,000 students and young men left their schools and their jobs to join his march. It will be a tough work, but fascinating. If we stick together and follow God's lead with boldness we shall win the world.

ALBERTO KOWARICK, *of the Kowarick Textile firm (Lanificio F. Kowarick, S.A.) of Sao Paulo, Latin America's largest city, was educated there and at Philadelphia Textile Institute in the United States. After ten years in industry, concerned by Brazil's growing political and social turmoil, he relinquished his major business responsibilities in order to devote himself to bringing about a revolution of national character and purpose throughout the continent. Kowarick is an enthusiastic yachtsman, and has won many prizes in horsemanship. He is a co-founder with Air Marshal Antonio Guedes Muniz of the Inter-American Center for Moral Re-Armament at Petropolis, Brazil, and was director of the Hemisphere Youth Demonstration at Rio de Janeiro in July, 1965. Mr. Kowarick, 37, is married to the former Anita Friele of New York. They have three children.*

7

MIRACLE IN BRAZIL

by

Alberto Kowarick

MY COUNTRY BRAZIL is a giant of a nation. Before Alaska was added to the United States we were the world's largest— after Russia, China and Canada. We occupy physically nearly half the South American continent and supply half its population. Our Amazon area alone is larger than the whole of Europe.

Brazil is a country with tremendous riches. It has the world's greatest hydro-electric potential, the world's biggest iron-ore deposits, 16% of the earth's forests, and immense reserves of oil, rubber and bauxite.

With all this wealth there is also appalling poverty. Millions starve at the doors of plenty. With resources to feed a population of 800 million people, we have a population of only 80 million, and two-thirds of them don't get enough to eat. Of Rio de Janeiro's four million inhabitants, one million live in slums.

For years, as a result of these social and economic contradictions, violent revolution has been boiling beneath the surface, and when Castro emerged on the Latin American scene he immediately became a hero to millions of my countrymen. Communist influence grew so that during the last days of Joao Goulart's Presidency a year and a half ago, its followers were virtually in control of the government.

You all know what happened then. The patriots of Brazil, especially the women and the military, decided that drastic action was needed. President Castelo Branco took over and began a "national revolution" that stopped the swing to the left and began a painful but long-needed process of recovery and reform. Much of this story has been well told in *Reader's Digest* under the title "The Country that Saved Itself."

This recovery still has a long way to go. In fact the hardest battles probably lie ahead. But a foundation has been laid, and if we all do our part, a new day will surely come for Brazil and all Latin America.

One of the most important factors in our national revolution is what has been happening in the docks of Brazil—the nation's lungs—and I want to tell you about it.

A year ago the Minister of Transport, on national television, had told a story of total breakdown and administrative anarchy in the Ports of Rio, Recife and Porte Alegre which were losing one and a half billion cruzeiros a month. Amazon basin ports were losing more money than the entire state budgets for the region. Coast-wise traffic had dropped to the lowest level for 40 years.

On May Day this year *Diario de Noticias,* Rio de Janeiro's biggest morning daily, distributed a 32-page supplement on national recovery. Six of its pages were given to the ports of Brazil. Some of the headlines read: "Total recuperation in last 11 months in Recife port"; "Records broken in Port of Rio"; "We're exporting answers, not problems."

Behind this startling economic transformation is the personal transformation in scores of dockers' leaders and men—a number of them former Communists—whose lives and purposes have been redirected by Moral Re-Armament. It all began in 1961 when an international force of Brazilian army officers, workers, industrialists and students, spearheaded by the Japanese play *The Tiger,* visited the chief centers of Brazil, Peru, Bolivia and Chile. The Japanese cast were composed of former Zengakuren students who had helped keep President Eisenhower out of Japan in the Tokyo riots the year before, and who through MRA had changed their attitude to America, made amends to Eisenhower and given their lives to what they called "a greater revolution."

The popular reception of *The Tiger* in Brazil was overwhelming. Hundreds of thousands of workers and peasants, including thousands of rank-and-file Communists flocked to see it. At Manaus up the Amazon, on the anniversary of Castro's revolution, a Communist rally drew an audience of 44. Across the way on a football field 90,000 cheered the Japanese. Later at San Marcos University, Peru, where Vice-President Nixon and Adlai Stevenson had received a hostile reception, students cheered *The Tiger,* wrote their own play *El Condor* on the causes and cure of anti-Americanism, and took it on tour across the continent and abroad.

The effect of these actions was summed up last July by President Castelo Branco in welcoming Peter Howard on his visit to the continent: "This extraordinary work has captured the workers, students and intellectuals of Brazil."

It was these workers who were chiefly responsible for the miracle of the docks. Two of them, Jarbas Leiros and Antonio Falcao of Recife were secretaries of the under-cover Communist cell in the port. Jarbas had planned to put an end to U.S. aid by dynamiting a food ship across the entrance to Recife harbor. They and many of their Communist colleagues left the Party after seeing the MRA force in action. Instead of opposing the Government and sabotaging American aid, they now threw their energies into ending the chaos and building a new spirit throughout the area. Today they are in responsible positions in the port. Polinice Xavier, their former deadly enemy, works with them in his position as head of the Union. He, like Falcao, gives a day's wages a month to help carry forward the program of MRA.

The Port Superintendent, Major Albuquerque, sees the need to deal with problems in men as his top priority, even before the need for new machinery. "We had to eradicate five things," he told the press, "corruption, subversion, false political promises, idleness and incompetence." Men responded with new productivity. The port, which in March 1964 showed a deficit of 230,000,000 cruzeiros, showed a profit balance of 2,500,000,000 cruzeiros in March 1965. In April 1965, all portworkers began receiving a production bonus which has raised their wages 50% to 60%. Money is at last available for the urgently needed re-equipping of the port, which should further improve efficiency.

MRA films were shown to hundreds of portworkers. "This spirit must go not only to every section of the port, but to every part of the city and state," said the Superintendent. On his insistence, the portworkers have been taking their films and experiences to all who work in the state railways, the textile factories and the sugar refineries.

Naval Captain Alvaro Calheiros, "Captain of the Ports," who is responsible for national security in the dock area says, "MRA has been proved effective in creating a new leadership."

Twenty-five hundred miles to the South is Rio Grande do Sul State, richest in wheat and beef. Gregorio Nascimento, who heads the dockers of Porto Alegre, the State capital, was considered a dangerous agitator and jailed by the new government during the days of crisis in April 1964. In August, a few months later, he presided at a meeting in his union hall at which portworkers from Rio de Janeiro spoke and showed films of an answer to hate and corruption. At the end of two hours he rose to reply. Sticking a fistful of notes into his hat he said, "We gaucho portworkers take our stand for a new Brazil through MRA. I want everyone to put a contribution in the hat to carry forward this mission." His bitterness was cured.

In February 1965, State Governor Menneghetti of Rio Grande do Sul said, "The first effects of that work are already beginning to be felt. For the first time in years, we are exporting meat to Recife from Rio Grande do Sul by ship, paying 42,000 cruzeiros a ton freight, instead of 120,000 cruzeiros a ton by truck. The meat arrives faster by ship, and there is no stealing."

A similar transformation took place in the port of Rio de Janeiro. In May 1964, Otton Barbosa, a tally-clerk and one of the founders of the Brazilian Socialist Party, was fed-up. During the years 1962-64 there had been so much corruption and subversion in the Port that men were ashamed to admit they were port-workers. A hundred and forty trained Communist agents had been moved into the docks with full government backing, and paid high overtime bonuses for their full-time ideological activities. They had put an end to many years of strike-free work and democratic union activities.

Then Barbosa went into action. "We are going to show that the vast majority of dockers want to give a fair day's work for a fair day's pay, and play their part in making Brazil a great nation," he said. He began showing MRA films in the warehouses during working hours. A minority sneered. But the mass response was enthusiastic. It vindicated Otton's theory that 90% were ready to sacrifice for the sake of the country, instead of sacrificing the country to their selfishness, and were only waiting for an honest and courageous lead.

As a result the Minister of Transport nominated Otton as Inspector in the key 1st Inspectorate (division) where 1,000 men work. It is called the "visitor's room" of the port, because it is there that the big transatlantic liners dock.

Otton accepted his appointment on one condition: that his policy would be based on applying absolute standards of conduct in every area and with everybody—both important men and ordinary men. He made this known to all concerned, inviting them to help him clean up the Inspectorate from top to bottom.

Many volunteered immediately. Corruption had become wide-spread—and not only amongst the portworkers. It had become routine for many shipping agents to send down envelopes of money for chiefs of sections and key workers such as crane-drivers, so as to get special treatment for their ships. Otton and his colleagues declared publicly that they would accept no bribes from anyone. The new Superintendent let it be known that any agent offering bribes would be barred from using port facilities. The Trans-Atlantic Shipping Center circulated all members, asking their co-operation in eliminating corruption.

Rio de Janeiro is the third largest coffee exporting port of Brazil, and 90% of that coffee passes through the 1st Inspectorate. The country had been losing huge dollar earnings through large-scale contraband in coffee. Otton's team worked out a new way of operating, with effective control, which eliminated coffee contraband in the area.

After three weeks Otton Barbosa was able to declare, "90% of the men of this Inspectorate are co-operating in creating a new sound climate. Formerly, when more than 15 crane crews were needed it was necessary to requisition extra workers. Now 23, 25 and 27 cranes can be worked at the same time using only the personnel of the Inspectorate, thus reducing enormously the operating costs."

These men have ended unfair privileges. Formerly, a small group of "blue-eyed boys" used to let the day-work go by and wait to be given overtime work at double pay. Now everyone gets equal treatment. Other Inspectorates are accepting the challenge of the leadership of "No. 1." In the Air Cargo division, for example, the newly-appointed warehouse chief, working on the basis of MRA, brought more money into the port coffers in his first month's work than had been collected in three months under the previous administration.

When the Minister of Transport brought these facts to the attention of President Castelo Branco in March of this year, Otton was promoted to be Director of Traffic, responsible for the whole port. The men of his old Inspectorate proudly point out that the new spirit is carried forward, not only by their new chief, who rose from the ranks, but by the mass of workers at all levels who want to create a decent country and a decent world.

PHYLLIS KONSTAM *studied for the theatre in London and Paris. She first went on the stage at the age of seventeen. She appeared in plays by Galsworthy and Shaw, played opposite Laurence Olivier on Broadway, and returning to London played leading roles in films directed by Alfred Hitchcock. With the outbreak of the Second World War she says, "I came to realize the deeper responsibility of artists towards their public." Later, in collaboration with British dramatist Peter Howard, she began to pioneer a theatre of faith, humanity and hope, developing the constructive function of stage and screen in the re-ordering of modern society. Miss Konstam is leading lady of the permanent Company of the Westminster Theatre. She is married to H. W. (Bunny) Austin, British Davis Cup tennis star, who is a trustee of the Westminster. They have a son and a daughter.*

8

THE RESPONSIBILITY
OF THE ARTIST

by

Phyllis Konstam

THE ARTIST has achieved immense influence in our society. He has also got away with a great big, fat confidence trick.

He has sold the public the idea that because he is an artist he doesn't have to be responsible. He can do whatever he likes, create whatever he likes, and nobody must interfere with him. And he is the only member of society who thinks he can get away with that kind of nonsense.

What would you feel about a baker who baked bad bread because he felt like it? What would happen if a butcher one day decided that he would sell the public contaminated meat because that is the way he felt about the customers? Supposing a doctor made all kinds of experiments on human beings because he felt he should be free in the sphere of science to try out new techniques on his patients. Wouldn't there soon be a public outcry, and wouldn't there be immediate action taken to prevent that kind of irresponsibility?

The artist, up to now, has got away with it because in a way he has been able to, because his sphere of things up to 30 years ago has been comparatively small. But with the coming of mass media—press, television, motion pictures—the entertainment world has moved into an entirely new dimension, comparable to the difference between the bow-and-arrow age and present-day nuclear power. Out of that small television box in the sitting room, in every village and city, ideas pour forth which condition the living and thinking of mankind.

The artist likes to think of himself as adult and advanced. In fact, many of us are children playing with very dangerous toys for our own pleasure and satisfaction, thinking only of expressing ourselves and not of the effect and consequences of what we do. A girl I spoke to here yesterday said, "The dramatist has a great time expressing himself but we, the younger generation, have to pay the price."

The trouble with so many artists at the present time is that they are tremendously self-centered. Recently I read an interview with a famous European film director. He had made a film so foul but so potent that the authorities had to close the boxes and balconies because of the devastating effect on the young people who saw it. The interviewer asked him what he felt the effect of this film would be on the millions who would eventually see it. Do you know what he replied? He said, "I never thought about it."

I am sure that is true. Many artists do not think. They think only of their art, their career, their productions. They feel in no way responsible for their actions. They have no sense of responsibility for the youth of their country or the world. Now that is not maturity, it is not adult, it is childish. A child doesn't think beyond its immediate action. An adult does or should, and that is the difference.

As I listened the other morning to Mr. Quinn Tamm, Director of the International Chiefs of Police, speaking of the outbreak of savagery and violence among young people all over the globe, I thought to myself, "We in the entertainment world stand guilty before God of corrupting a whole generation." Violence, moral anarchy and godlessness has poured forth from stage, screen and television year in, year out, and it has had a most devastating effect on young and old alike.

Today the fashion in our country is the theatre of cruelty, perversion and nihilism. Life is made out to be a meaningless, bad joke. Dramatists who like to think of themselves as avant-garde are, in fact, avant garbage. They slop their filthy refuse over the heads of the public and label it great art. Why should dirty homes and slum areas be looked on as an evil and a sore in society, and dirty minds be looked on as advanced and progressive?

Someone asked me today about the theatre of the absurd. All I can say is that I find it enormously depressing. I cannot think plays are a good thing that leave you wanting to commit suicide. I talked to a well-known English doctor not very long ago, and he told me that in the hospital where he was a consultant there were a stream of would-be suicides brought in, many of them

60

teen-agers. He said he made it his job to sit by the bed of these young people to find out what made them want to kill themselves. He said there were many contributing factors, but one of the most important, they said, was that at the end of a difficult day, to see a frightfully depressing and meaningless play was the last straw, making them feel there was no meaning to life any more.

I am absolutely certain that teen-agers are doing some of the things they are doing in my country because they constantly see cruel plays and films. It becomes a way of life. It doesn't seem terrible any more. Recently some of our young people threw an old man over a pier, and when the judge asked them why they did it, they said, "Well after all, we didn't kill him, he was only bruised."

But even more serious than the dirt, perversion and sadism, is the godlessness, the deliberate attempt to destroy our faith. For destroy God, and every evil can be rationalized and the cruelty latent in every heart will be unleashed. The values of the artist are of the greatest importance, because he sets a fashion which the whole country will eventually follow.

The Communists have understood, as we have not, the power and influence of the theatre. The first thing to be taken over in Red China was the theatre, and plays are used there to indoctrinate people all across the land. From Moscow companies go out and indoctrinate the farm workers, and go right through the rural areas of Russia. In Vietnam, Vietcong troops move into villages, put on plays and disappear again. They use them to train the millions. In the western world the man who has most affected drama today is Bertolt Brecht—a committed Communist who decided he would use the theatre to change society. His influence on culture has been immense. He has created a new trend.

The original Greek theatre had a great purpose. It was part of the character-building process for the nation, and as you know, plays originally were compulsory for the whole community. Shakespeare's plays, too, do not always come out very happily in the end, but you see the consequences of evil. In a play like *Hamlet*, for instance, you see what happens when people take the wrong course. And Shakespeare wrote "the play's the thing with which to catch the conscience of the King."

George Bernard Shaw, describing the aims of the theatre, said it must be "a prompter of conscience, an elucidator of social conduct, an armory against despair and dullness, and a temple of the ascent of man."

61

Today we need actors, dramatists and directors who will start a new trend; artists who dare to say that hate is curable, passion can be redirected, that man is not only capable of sinking to great depths but also of rising to great heights; artists who love God and do not spit in His face. There is a hunger deep in the heart of every man for great living. Let us for Heaven's sake feed that hunger and not gorge him on things which create a sick society.

Lenin once said, "There is a plank inside the brain of every Englishman through which no new idea can pass." I believe that applies to many artists. They cannot believe, despite the heights artists have often attained in the past, that they are capable of even greater heights; that we have not yet seen the new horizons which the great Creator Himself can open up for us if we are humble enough truly to seek His inspiration.

I believe that in the new, fascinating, but dangerous age in which we find ourselves, when it is possible to destroy all life on this planet, the creative artist must find a new sense of responsibility. He must use his God-given gifts, not to lure us down the road to destruction, but to show us the way out of our problems and lead us into the new society we all long for.

Let us find young artists who dare to speak up for what is right, and refuse to be silenced or blackmailed by the vocal minority who are resolved that vice rather than virtue shall flourish, and godlessness rather than faith shall be our way of life.

Now I want to speak about Peter Howard.

I am a woman of the theatre. It has been my profession for over forty years. I do not say this lightly, but I am sure that when the history of the theatre comes to be written, Peter Howard will stand out as a giant among men. While so many small, self-centered dramatists were obsessed with sex and perversion and did not care that millions went hungry or homeless, or that bands of young people roamed the country bored and without purpose or faith, while they wrote plays which flew a banner for one class or one race, there stood a man, firm as a rock, who cared for all men.

Peter Howard did not think of people as upper class or middle class or lower class, as black, white, brown or yellow. He thought of them as men and he loved them. That is why there echoed round the world after he died, "He was our friend." And he was. He cared for the boss and the worker, the young and the old. He carried humanity on his heart, and he wrote with a passion to put right the wrongs of our society.

62

"He was like a Cedar of Lebanon amidst a lot of underbrush," said Cardinal Cushing. "He was determined that goodness should not perish from the earth," said Mr. Quintin Hogg, the British Cabinet Minister, at his memorial service. While other dramatists wrote meaningless, dirty, hopeless plays which destroy faith in God and in humanity, Peter Howard wrote of the answer available for all men. He turned man Godward in a godless age, and we and coming generations owe him an undying debt of gratitude. In these crucial days of history, when mankind's future literally hangs in the balance, I feel privileged beyond measure to have had a part in his plays and to be a member of the permanent company of the Westminster Theatre, which is the most courageous, intelligent and truly avant garde theatre of this century.

I believe together the artists of the world can create a theatre which answers the greed, hate, selfishness and lust in man which are the real roots of human misery and suffering. It is to a theatre of that dimension, dedicated to that mighty purpose, that we are meant to give our lives.

PROFESSOR RAMAKRISHNA VAITHESWARAN *of Hyderabad University, India, first came to public notice when he won a brilliant first place out of 22,000 candidates in the Indian Civil Service Examinations. Earlier, as an official of the Indian Communist Party, he was jailed for his leadership of guerrilla activities in central India and spent two and a half years in prison. After meeting Moral Re-Armament 12 years ago he left the Party and is now a close colleague of Rajmohan Gandhi in his campaign for national renewal. Professor Vaitheswaran is 35, married, with two daughters.*

9

HOW TO WIN ASIA

by

Ramakrishna Vaitheswaran

TWICE recently the United States has had to intervene with her armed strength to prevent a possible Communist takeover—first in Vietnam, then in the Dominican Republic. In Vietnam, U.S. arms and troops are committed to an already massive extent, and by the inexorable logic of events, the commitment will grow more, not less, in the immediate days ahead.

Let there be no doubt about it, however much we may regret the horrors of continued war, that this American action safeguards the nations of South and Southeast Asia, for the time being, from Chinese Communist advance. But let there be no doubt, as well, that long-term effectiveness in achieving the aims of this country and the desires of the peoples of Asia will depend on whether the non-Communist nations and the United States find common ideological goals that go beyond national interests.

There is a powerful and vocal, if only a minority, opinion in your country that argues and demonstrates against your government's present policy. These so-called liberals are supported and reinforced by many powerful forces, including government, in Asia. They want a withdrawal of the U.S. presence from my part of the world. They console themselves with the possibility that Ho Chi-minh will emerge as an anti-Chinese Tito. They present what they call "National Communism" as a desirable end of policy. I have no doubt that those who say this today about Vietnam will say it tomorrow about Thailand, Burma, India, Pakistan and Ceylon. This attitude considers some form of dictatorship as inevitable for the masses of Asia.

As an Asian, I refuse to accept that the choice for us is only between two kinds of Communism. Even in Vietnam, if the United States will acknowledge the mistakes of her past Vietnamese policy, she will begin to repair the damage. If she backs this up by giving Moral Re-Armament to the fighting soldiers of both the U.S. and South Vietnam, it can turn an otherwise hopeless situation.

What are the facts?

1. President Ho Chi-minh accepted partition in Geneva at the 17th parallel purely as a temporary measure to consolidate North Vietnam and regroup forces in the South.

2. The Delta area of Cochin-China had always been the stronghold of the Communist Party of Vietnam and President Ho Chi-minh anticipated victory at the elections scheduled to be held in the whole of Vietnam in 1956.

3. When it became clear that there was going to be no peaceful takeover through an election, North Vietnam regrouped, organized and supported guerrilla activity in the South in a bid to take over violently.

4. The strength of the North has been a basic cadre of dedicated people in the South, who have a base in the villages. The base is maintained partly by terror but also partly by the support the Communists have won among certain classes of the rural population.

5. The Diem government initially had a certain mass base in the villages, though this became difficult to maintain under conditions of Viet Cong terror. At a certain stage, the late President realized he would have to reinforce military measures with a "saturation campaign" for Moral Re-Armament to inspire the masses to an ideological loyalty similar to that of the Communists. But the American government discouraged him even as they had condemned him for his weaknesses. Personal incompatibilities and irritations were allowed to encourage the exit of Diem. Mao Tse-tung in his recent interview with Edgar Snow has expressed the amazement of the Chinese at the American attitude to Diem. This mistake, which the so-called liberals helped to foster, is now being paid for in blood.

6. For a long time subsequent governments, relying for their power almost exclusively on cliques of army officers, had neither the will nor the ability even to consider securing popular support.

7. Partly as a result of her own mistakes, the United States has had to fight the war in Vietnam virtually as an occupying power. This is a logical consequence of the U.S. desire to make the combat

decisions which Diem, as a self-respecting nationalist ruler, insisted on making himself.

8. President Johnson decided to make up for the weakness of the American political and ideological position by overwhelming military strength. But the local population were terrorized or unsympathetic, and the South Vietnamese were demoralized by the power struggle of their officers. In this situation, pitched against an elusive, all-pervading enemy who fought on his own conditions at his own timing, military strength was and is limited in what it can do.

9. The strength of the Communist position is that they still have the ability to win men to their ideology, and the leadership to carry out their strategy.

10. The weakness of the American position is the inability even to keep the friends this nation once had, let alone obtain an understanding of its policies, or the Asian leadership to carry them out.

The last is the crux of the matter. The attitude of calling the tune as well as paying the piper is bound to lead to conflict with every sensitive nationalist, just as it did with Diem. Realizing this, the tendency at present seems to be to base policy on strength, and not on winning support or friends. It is true that this policy is softened by promises of economic aid. But it seems the United States has given up any hope of finding understanding for her policies, and is therefore determined to pursue them undeterred.

To a certain extent, this new firmness is preferable to the old kowtowing to every Asian or African who called himself a nationalist. But I am convinced that the increasing tendency to rely on force and pressure will be self-defeating. The failure to win other nations ideologically may result in a still more dangerous neo-isolationism, and eventually a frustrated abdicating of America's world responsibility.

In my own country, India, I have met in the past weeks great resentment at what is called the pushing and the pressuring. A few days before I left New Delhi I asked an influential policy-maker of our government the explanation for the present bad state of Indo-U.S. relations. His reply was, "President Johnson does not make it easy for us to be friends with him." Another man who was concerned for a number of years with vital decisions of foreign policy shouted, "If only they would leave us alone."

Of course, these men were in a state of reaction. They are probably difficult men. It is not easy to make friends with the sensitive but demanding nationalists of newly independent countries. Often their fixed prejudices and preconceived notions must be exasperating to the representatives of this country. But there is no short cut to dealing with people: winning them, changing them, establishing a basis for a common ideology with them.

It is possible, of course, to change Communists, and there is no reason why Americans should not be changing them all the time.

Take myself as an example. I belong to a lower middle-class family in India. I studied until my university M.A. without an electric light. I studied by a hurricane lantern. I had food, clothing, and so forth. But very early in my life I became aware of a distinction between myself and my father's friends who were slightly better off.

I used to go to college without proper clothes and people used to laugh at me, thinking, "Aha! This bookworm doesn't really know how to dress." Something hardened inside me and I thought, "One day I'll show these so-and-so's what kind of person I am."

I am a Brahmin. In the Hindu religion, Brahmin is the priestly community, the highest caste. Quite a number of the Brahmins talk about religion and God but act like hypocrites. I saw that my own community made religion into a profession. Karl Marx wrote that religion is the opiate of the people and the instrument of the upper class to exploit the lower classes. I thought, "That is true about my own community. That is what we are doing with these masses of people."

When I learned about Marxism, I read quite a number of the books of Karl Marx and Lenin. Two things attracted me about them: 1. The vision of a new type of society without any kind of exploitation. 2. A method by which I take part in creating a new type of society.

Here I am, I thought, a part of the inevitable process of history. That is how I became a Communist.

I took part in an armed struggle against the landlords of my state in South India, and was put in jail for two-and-a-half years. In jail we were often starved, sometimes beaten. There were shootings, and a number of my comrades of that time died in front of me. These things only made me more bitter. I also had the chance to study and train myself in jail. When I came out, I was a more bitter, more determined, better-trained Communist than when I went in.

A little after that I met Moral Re-Armament. The first man I met was an Englishman. He said, "I regret the wrongs my country has done to your country, and wish to take full responsibility for them." I said, "This is the first time that any man, let alone an Englishman, has apologized to me for anything."

Indians, you know, never apologize. There are certain things we cannot say. One is, "You have done well, congratulations." Another is, "I'm sorry."

I was very impressed by this Englishman. I got to know him well. He told me how every morning you can sit quietly and listen to your inner voice or conscience. I liked the idea because I wanted to do well and correct my mistakes. Even though I didn't believe in God, I believed in conscience, and got thoughts which helped me in my work.

For the first time since I joined the Party I began to question my basis of life. Until then I had a wonderful image of myself as a self-sacrificing, dedicated Party fighter. Then one night at a conference like this I lay awake and thought, "Have I done all the things I should have done? Have I avoided all the things I should not have done?" And, quite simply, the picture I had of myself began to alter. I thought I was a man who cared for other people. I thought I had sacrificed a lot. But I saw that I had also wanted, deeply wanted, power. I thought I cared for other people, but I realized that I used them.

I came to a conference of Moral Re-Armament in Switzerland. I came as a Communist. At this conference I saw clearly that although I had started as an idealist who wanted a new type of society, because I was ambitious and bitter and had used ambition and bitterness as an instrument for my revolution, I had ended up a ruthless man with all the elements in my make-up that would turn me into a Stalin if I had power.

Just as there can be capitalistic exploiters, there can also be Communist exploiters whose basis of exploitation is different. This basis is power. We get power and use it ruthlessly. I saw this and I realized that Communism can never create a new type of society unless it has the secret of answering the ambitions, the bitterness and moral compromise in men like me. Otherwise we end up by becoming exploiters.

Moral Re-Armament confronts Communists with the gap between what they say about a new society without exploitation, and what they actually do. When they see the gap and a way of bridging it, they see Moral Re-Armament is a higher stage than Communism.

There are thousands of Communists who have been won over.

One of them, Hans Bjerkholt of Norway, founded the Communist Party in his country. He used to take part in the deliberations at the Kremlin of the Executive Committee of the Comintern. He said that there was one problem on the agenda that was never solved: how to create a new type of man. "We Communists failed to do it," he said. "Moral Re-Armament is doing it."

I started on the road to change through Moral Re-Armament because I met Westerners who were living in a way that made me want to be like them. It was a level of revolutionary unselfishness beyond what I had seen in any Communist. I knew instinctively that the idea which had captured them must be very powerful indeed.

It is strange but true that the Communists, who are pure materialists, attach far more importance than non-Communists to the power of ideas to capture men, the grandeur of aim to inspire people to great deeds, and the example of dedicated living to evoke a degree of heroism and self-sacrifice. Your job and mine is to furnish idea, aim and example to democracy.

I have come to the conclusion that the lack of enthusiasm for, and scepticism about ideology among intellectuals and policy-makers of the non-Communist world comes from a reluctance to match the moral heritage of democracy with great living. America shares with many nations, certainly with my own, a dislike of the discomfort of uncompromising living, and a determination to rationalize the gods of affluence, sex and personal success. Thank God that modern youths are rejecting these values of an older generation.

Our common aim must be to make sure that the aid generously supplied by American taxpayers to keep countries like mine going is in fact effective; that the lives and blood of American soldiers sacrificed on Asian soil do in fact secure your objectives and purposes. But we must make this nation understand that the injection of dollars into a tottering economy, important as it is, is not a substitute for leadership that will evoke the sacrifice and sweat of the nations concerned. Armed strength, necessary as it is, is not a substitute for ideological weakness. Power and pressure are not a substitute for persuasion. There is in fact no alternative to Moral Re-Armament.

The most important question of our time is not Russia or China, or the course of events in Asia or Africa, but whether or not the U.S.A. has an ideology which she will bring to bear on her relations with all these nations.

I was asked today what, from the point of view of an Asian, are the most important ingredients in a successful American policy for Asia.

First, I think, is to have it run by men who care for people and are sensitive to them. Such men will realize that if Asia needs America, America also needs Asia. They will treat both cabinet officials and the ordinary people of Asia and Africa in a different way. They will understand them, try and win them, and not dictate to them.

Second, is to have something to say—to know what is America's message to Asia. If such a question is asked of a Russian, he will immediately reply, "This is what I am going to say." The Russian has a message for our continent. What is America's message? Think about that. It's a very, very important question.

Third, is the way Americans live abroad. I was in Vietnam some time ago and met American soldiers. They were first-class men, but like soldiers everywhere many had mistresses. Think of the bitterness this creates. I love America, and I say these things because I want the very best for her. I want her representatives to give the right leadership to Asia. I would advise all American officials abroad, "Train your people in how to live. If you do, you will win the respect and gratitude of Asia and Africa, and the rest of the world besides."

RICHARD PRINCE OF HESSE, *son of the late Land-grave Frederik Charles of Hesse, is a member of one of Europe's oldest Royal Houses dating back to the ninth century. On his mother's side he is a nephew of Kaiser Wilhelm II and a grandson of Queen Victoria of England. Prince Richard is a Director of the German Council for Moral Re-Armament and of the Caux Foundation in Switzer-land. A life-long specialist in motor transport, he is Chairman of the Board of the Road Safety Council for the State of Hesse, and Vice-Chairman for the Federal Republic of Germany. His home is at Kronberg Castle in the Taunus Mountains near Frankfurt-on-Main.*

10

HANDS ACROSS THE RHINE

by

Richard Prince of Hesse

A FORTNIGHT ago I was having dinner with one of Germany's most popular men, Joseph Neckerman, owner of the largest mail-order firm in the country. The firm has a slogan: "Neckerman machts moeglich" (Neckerman makes anything possible.) Everybody in Germany knows that slogan.

Neckerman is also a great sportsman who has won gold medals at three Olympics. He talked about his experiences in Tokyo last year and Rome four years earlier. What struck me most was what he said about the American athletes. He said that in Rome they had not impressed him at all. They had been loud, undisciplined and generally out to amuse themselves and do things they had better not have done. Their reputation was not good.

At Tokyo four years later it was exactly the opposite. The Americans were the most disciplined and serious of all the Olympic teams. They were not only out to win, but to represent their country in the best possible way. This had interested him very much and he couldn't explain it.

I was able to help him out, for I told him about the two United States athletes who had been at Rome, had afterwards met Moral Re-Armament, and last autumn helped train the American team before they went to Tokyo. They are here with us—"Rusty" Wailes and John Sayre.

I had the great luck of being one of the first to meet Frank Buchman, who began Moral Re-Armament. It was soon after the First World War, at a hotel in Lucerne, Switzerland. I was 19 then, and Frank must have been twice my age. He was quite unknown. Nobody had ever heard his name or knew what he stood for. He

73

spoke of a certain work he was doing, but I could never quite take in what he meant. My head was full of girls and other things.

We got to be good friends and Frank was able to help me in a mess I got into once. As the years went on he came to see my family and me regularly every year in Germany. We always looked forward to those visits. We used to call them the "Buchman Season." Then I learned he knew people in many countries and had friends living everywhere. He told us about many parts of the world that he had been to. He was usually just back from China or Latin America or Africa or some other place.

In 1933 the Nazi regime in Germany began. He came to the Olympics in 1936, and to one of the National Socialist rallies at Nuremberg, attended by all the foreign diplomats. He watched the rise of the two great totalitarian ideologies, Nazism and Communism, both of which were materialistic and lacked moral foundations. He saw the struggle between them, and the ineffective efforts of the western democracies, which were themselves quite materialistic in practice, to deal with either of them.

It must have been about this time that Frank Buchman, realizing that democracy as then practised was failing, as totalitarianism had failed, to give nations what they needed, conceived the idea that the next big move in the world must be a moral action on a massive scale—a moral ideology. Everywhere at that time military rearmament was in the air, and he called his idea Moral Re-Armament. He conceived it in 1938 at Freudenstadt, in the Black Forest of Germany, where he used to go occasionally for a rest.

Shortly after that, as we know, the Second World War broke out and five and a half years of total war ended with the complete collapse of the Nazi dictatorship. Germany was practically wiped out. Nothing functioned any more. There was no government, no nation, and only a third of what had been German territory was left to us. Nobody knew what was going to happen. The Western Allies—England, France and the United States—were trying to find a way of doing something with Germany. They thought she might be re-educated, but nobody knew how that was to be done.

Three important events for Germany took place after the Second World War, and they all had something to do with MRA.

First was the establishment of the international training center at Caux, Switzerland. In 1946 the former Caux Palace Hotel, located high above Lake Geneva at one of the most famous beauty spots in Europe, was purchased by the Swiss and put at Frank

Buchman's disposal. When he arrived there for the opening of the first World Assembly for Moral Re-Armament his first question was, "Where are the Germans?" Of course no Germans had been invited because Germans at that time could not leave Germany. We could not get passports, the Swiss would not give us visas, and there was no money to travel. But Frank had his own ideas about Germany—even about the destroyed, disillusioned and outlawed people that we then were. For after all Germany was still the heart of Europe.

If you look at the map, Europe reaches from the west coast of Spain to the Ural Mountains in Russia. It is a fact many people don't realize. The only statesman who mentions it, interestingly enough, is De Gaulle. Many seem to think that Europe ends on the Eastern border of Germany. But Frank Buchman saw Europe as he had always known it, with Germany in the center, and he said, "You can't rebuild Europe without Germany."

Soon after that the American Occupation Commander, General Clay, was interviewed in Berlin, and made arrangements for a delegation of leading Germans to go to Caux. The Swiss Government agreed to give them visas, and the Swiss and one or two farsighted Americans put up the necessary funds.

So in 1947 and 1948 large groups of Germans came to Caux for training. Most of them were government people, politicians, leaders of political parties, big business leaders and leaders of the labor unions. For a dozen years Germany had been isolated from the rest of the world. Few contacts had been possible. Nobody had been out of Germany, and very few foreigners had been inside. Now for the first time in many years Germans were received as equals.

The United States had generously helped us through the Marshall Plan to rebuild our cities and our economy. But Frank Buchman thought that more was needed. He remembered the chaos following the First World War when few people except the Communists troubled their heads over what was really going on in Germany. As a result the situation went from bad to worse, and eventually the Nazis took over. Frank well knew that if the Germans were again left to themselves, the country would go Communist.

By inviting Germans to Caux, Frank Buchman made them feel that they were again part of the family of nations, and Caux became, as Dr. Adenauer has said, a "household word" in post-war Germany.

The second event took place in the Ruhr, which is the big

industrial area of Germany. You must remember that during the Nazi reign everyone opposed to National Socialism either fled the country or were put into concentration camps, particularly Jews and Communists. Many Jews in the concentration camps were murdered—a crime that will always remain on the conscience of my country.

After the war the survivors were naturally not interested in going back to Germany. The Communists were different because they had a purpose. Many of them had fled to Russia. Now they flocked back to their old homes. They wanted to build a Communist Germany. They had an idea to fight for.

In those days in the Ruhr, the proportion of Communist votes in the Works Councils of the coal and steel industries amounted to over 72 per cent. Dr. Adenauer, by then Chancellor, and Karl Arnold, Minister President for the State of North-Rhine-Westphalia where the Ruhr is situated, had been to Caux, and they invited an MRA force to Germany.

The MRA team lived in the Ruhr for months. They stayed with the miners in their homes. And the people of the Ruhr, who before had only heard first Nazi and then Communist propaganda, began to be gripped by something new—an idea for everybody and not only for one class or one race. Even leaders of the Communist Party began to be interested. Some of them went to Caux and came back changed men. That worried the Party leaders. They sent more men to investigate, including Party officials. When these also came back changed from Caux, it was finally decided to expel 40 top Communists from the Party.

Meanwhile the Communist vote in the Works Councils fell in three years from 72% to 25% and even lower. The Ruhr was not taken over by Communism, as it had been feared, and much of the credit for this result must go to the men of Moral Re-Armament.

The third event of those days was even more important. You all know that Germany and France have been fighting each other for centuries. I remember being taught at school in Germany before the First World War that the French were our arch-enemies. The hatred goes back hundreds of years. In the 17th and 18th centuries French troops often fought on German soil, and many of the ruined German castles one sees along the banks of the Rhine were ruined in those wars. During the French Revolution, French armies invaded Germany and seized the left bank of the Rhine. Later Napoleon and his enormous army crossed the borders and controlled the whole of Central Europe, including Germany. Then in 1870 it was the other way round—German troops invaded France. In the First and Second World Wars France was again invaded. There was reason enough for both sides to hate each other.

In those first post-war years Frank Buchman knew a famous French statesman, Robert Schuman, who had been Prime Minister of France and had resigned his post. They met in Paris just after Schuman's resignation and had a talk. Frank asked him, "What are you going to do now? Have you any plans for the future?" Schuman replied he wanted to have a rest and then thought of going to North Africa for a visit, and he had all kinds of invitations.

After a while he said, "I think there must be something else for me," and Frank nodded. Then Schuman said, "I know what you are thinking—it is the question of France and Germany somehow reuniting." Frank said, "Yes, and you're the man to do it." Schuman said, "Tell me how to do it. I don't know how." Frank answered, "Well, I can't tell you, but if you listen to God He will tell you what to do."

Later Robert Schuman asked Frank, "Can you tell me who are the Germans I can talk to about this? I don't know anybody in Germany." So Frank wrote down several names, among them that of Dr. Konrad Adenauer, soon to become German Chancellor.

Adenauer was a man who had always been interested in France. Already between the two World Wars he had tried unsuccessfully to find some way of getting France and Germany to be friends. Schuman had been born in Alsace, where people still speak German while being French, and he himself was bilingual. Now these two men met for the first time and started to work together on their long-cherished idea.

It didn't come off at once. But the Schuman Plan for merging the Iron and Steel industries of the two countries paved the way, and when Robert Schuman fell ill, others took up the work. Adenauer and De Gaulle became friends, and before Adenauer's retirement as Chancellor a treaty of friendship was signed between France and Germany, bringing a unity unknown since the time of Charlemagne a thousand years before.

Although with Adenauer's departure Franco-German relations lost something of their previous warmth, there is no longer hatred on either side between these ancient rivals—a fact not only of historic importance in itself, but one that gives promise of healing for all the other enmities with which our world is still divided.

PHILIPPE MOTTU *of Lausanne, Swiss sociologist,*
studied sociology and political science at the Uni-
versities of Geneva and Lausanne. During the last
war he was appointed by the Commander-in-Chief
to supervise ideological training for the French-
speaking units of the Swiss Army, and after three
years at the Foreign Office became a co-founder in
1946 of Moral Re-Armament's European center at
Caux-sur-Montreux. He has lectured widely on
both sides of the Atlantic, and is the author of
L'OCCIDENT AU DEFI (Challenge to the West), *and*
THE NECESSARY REVOLUTION. *M. Mottu, 52, is*
married and has a son and three daughters.

11

THE SECRET OF CIVILIZATION

by

Philippe Mottu

EVER SINCE boyhood one fact of history has fascinated my imagination. Why is it that nations, like people, are born, grow up, reach their peak, maintain themselves, and then decline and disintegrate. Change in nations, like change in men, is one of life's most absorbing realities.

My generation has known a Germany with a totalitarian state, concentration camps and an aggressive policy which nearly engulfed all Europe. How is it and why is it that Germany has been so fundamentally transformed in the last twenty years? You may see a similar change in Russia or China during your lifetime. Nations can change for better or for worse, and we must not commit the fundamental mistake of thinking that they stay forever the way they are today. Like a majestic river, history flows on, and each generation can alter its course by the way it lives and behaves.

What are the forces which preside over these monumental events in human society?

Already in 1734 Montesquieu, the famous French author of *The Greatness and Decadence of the Romans,* refused to follow Machiavelli, the famous Italian statesman who believed that *chance* rules the world.

Recently Toynbee, the great British historian, has tried to interpret the history of civilization by the tensions between what he called the challenge and the response. But his method explains more the *how* than the *why,* and does not reveal the inner secret of history.

In a series of lectures at the University of Vienna, Professor Sigmund Freud made an interesting remark: "We believe," he writes, "that civilization has been built up by sacrifices in the gratification of the primitive impulses, and that to a great extent it is being perpetually recreated as each individual repeats the sacrifice of his instinctive pleasures for the common good. The sexual are amongst the most important of the instinctive forces thus utilized; they are in this way sublimated—that is to say, their energy is turned aside from its sexual goal and diverted towards other ends, no longer sexual and socially more valuable."

This suggestion of Freud has been the basis of much research in recent decades, especially by the British sociologist J. D. Unwin. Thirty years ago he published a thick book of 676 pages which has not become a best-seller but is more and more referred to today.

Unwin made an extensive sociological inquiry into 80 primitive societies and 16 historical civilizations. His research was particularly directed toward the different ways of regulating the relationship between the two sexes, and the extraordinary parallel that exists between their social habits and the level of culture.

In the course of his inquiry Unwin proved in a most convincing manner that social rules which limit or prevent the immediate satisfaction of sexual desire create emotional tensions. These tensions, which are the source of the social energy of a human society, seem to be the driving force of a civilization. There appears to be a close relation between the limiting of sexual opportunity and the development of civilization.

Contrary to animals, which are regulated in a very strict way by instinct, man can control the sexual act by the free choice of his brain. The more complete the mastery of the sexual instinct, the more a man becomes human and gets away from the animal in him. The more that social rules and personal discipline make sexual intercourse difficult and rare, the more social energy is developed. This social energy is then used for social ends that are more useful and will develop civilization.

The opposite is also true. If rules and discipline are relaxed, if sexual relations become easier, then social energy diminishes and culture declines. The state of civilization of each human society at any given moment will depend, therefore, on the quality of social energy which it has at its disposal.

The facts show that societies which have less energy are those in which continence before marriage is not imposed and where opportunities to give in to sexual appetite are the greatest. Scientific research proves that continence is the source or basis of creative thinking, and that you get creative thinking after you have had continence, not the other way round.

We don't know exactly what social energy is, but we can see the fruits of it in the successive stages of development of a nation or civilization. The social system that requires chastity before marriage and fidelity inside marriage is the one which keeps to a minimum the opportunities for sexual relations. The documents at our disposal indicate that all the great civilizations have started their course on this basis. The introduction of the practice of continence in a society which is accustomed to sexual license, constitutes the most important and the most costly of social revolutions.

The first stage of social energy resulting from sexual continence expresses itself in a civilization in what can be called "Expansive" energy. States and societies so motivated become aggressive, they conquer their neighbors who are less energetic than they, they found colonies, they develop their trade and industry, they spend their energy in such activities.

If a strict tradition of sexual restraint continues for several generations, the resulting energy shows itself in a form which can be called productive energy. Such productive energy expresses itself in the form of science, theoretical research, art, and in the transformation of the social structure of society.

Ideas only become practical when people have the will to put them to work. You get the will as a result of personal discipline. Therefore ideas come to nothing unless you have morality. An idea only becomes an actual reality when social energy has been used to make it practical. A nation without sexual discipline will not have its ideas realized. If for many generations a society does not practice continence, its whole civilization collapses and is finally replaced by another society.

There are many very striking examples in history. One of them is Rome. After describing the sexual discipline and "expansive social energy" of the Romans who extended their sway over the whole of the Mediterranean area, rising from an insignificant township to a position of domination in less than three centuries, Dr. Unwin writes:

"It is difficult to imagine a more complete reduction of sexual opportunity or a more rigid cancellation of personal impulses. These men gave Rome her *gravitas*. Their honorable dealings became proverbial as the 'faith of the Romans,' which towards the end of the Republic disappeared."

By the end of the first century of our era we are told that "the Romans satisfied their sexual desires in a direct manner." Consequently they had no energy for anything else. The old traditions, however, were still preserved in some parts of the Empire, such as Illyria and Spain. Many of the provincials went to Rome and succeeded to high office, and it was these provincials who gave the Roman Empire strength.

"Then in their turn the provincials reversed the habits of their fathers by extending their sexual opportunity. The lack of energy displayed by their sons and grandsons is apparent in the records of the third century.

"Yet once more there emerged a group of men who had spent their early years in an atmosphere of compulsory continence. I mean the Christians. They had survived many violent persecutions; eventually they dominated the Empire, which in the fourth century recovered the strength it had shown in the second century. The Edict of Milan may have been a political move, but Constantine was right in thinking that the Christians were men on whom he should rely.

"Then the Christians in their turn changed their habits. In the matter of post-nuptial regulations they compromised with the civil authorities. Then the Teutons overran the Western Empire. These Teutons possessed, in regard to sexual regulations, the same absolute monogamous ideas that the Sumerians, Babylonians, Athenians and Romans had once possessed, and later discarded."

Other sociologists have come to exactly the same conclusions as Unwin. We could quote many of them, but I will simply mention the conclusion of Dr. P. A. Sorokin, for many years Chairman of the Sociology Department at Harvard University. In one of his recent books Professor Sorokin summarizes his conclusions on two principal ideas:

"1. The regime that confines sexual life within socially sanctioned marriage, and that morally disapproves and legally prohibits premarital and extramarital relations, provides an environment more favorable for the creative growth of society than does the regime of free or disorderly sex relationships which neither morally disapproves nor legally prohibits premarital and extramarital liaisons.

"2. The regime that permits chronically excessive, illicit, and disorderly sex activities contributes to the decline of cultural creativity."

Summarizing his findings, Dr. Unwin writes: "Sometimes a man has been heard to declare that he wishes both to enjoy the advantage of high culture and to abolish compulsory continence. The inherent nature of the human organism, however, seems to be such that these desires are incompatible, even contradictory. Any human society is free to choose either to display great energy or to enjoy sexual freedom; the evidence is that it cannot do both for more than one generation."

Everywhere in the world great dams are being built today to hold water which will be used for irrigation, or for production of the electric energy necessary for modern life. In the moral domain we follow the opposite road. We knock down one after the other all the dams, all the dikes, all the barricades which channel human liberty. This phenomenon is taking place at the precise moment when the will of man has become tremendously amplified because of the power of the machine over which he has dominion. A dam channels water to produce electricity. There is a striking parallel between these two kinds of energy. Any civilization which wants to maintain and develop a vital life will have to avoid wasting its sexual energy for selfish aims that have no social value.

The extraordinary development of science and modern techniques is in part due to the application of procedures that become more and more exact in their measurements, standards which become more and more precise because of modern instruments and machines. Why should not what is true in the realm of physical science be true also in the realm of the science of man and his life on this planet?

The energy produced by continence is not of course moral in itself. It can be used for different aims, and that is exactly what we find in history. Totalitarian regimes, like Nazism and Fascism, which enforced continence on people and combined it with a system of authoritarian education, produced a very energetic, military generation which was on the verge of dominating Europe.

Today for reasons that are easy to understand, the Chinese Communist Party has a similar philosophy: "Love between men and women is an activity which consumes much time and energy. Love of the masses, of the Party and of President Mao Tse-tung does not take any time. Try it. Your spirit will rise as well as your productivity, and you will be ten times more useful to the community."

An experiment carried out in the Soviet Union during the years immediately following the revolution is extremely interesting. Sorokin writes:

"During the first stage of the Revolution, its leaders deliberately attempted to destroy marriage and the family. Free love was glorified. The legal distinction between marriage and casual sexual intercourse was abolished. The Communist law spoke only of 'contracts' between males and females for the satisfaction of their desires either for an indefinite or a definite period —a year, a month, a week, or even for a single night. One could marry and divorce as many times as desired. Husband or wife could obtain a divorce without the other being notified. It was not even necessary that 'marriages' be registered. Abortion was facilitated in state institutions. Premarital relations were praised, and extramarital relations were considered normal.

"The old pragmatic test: 'By their fruits ye shall know them,' provides the answer to the question whether this sex freedom was practical. Within a few years, hordes of wild, homeless children became a menace to the Soviet Union itself. Millions of lives, especially of young girls, were wrecked; divorces skyrocketed, as did abortions. Work in the nationalized factories slackened.

"The total results were so appalling that the government was forced to reverse its policy. Free love was declared to be counter-revolutionary, and its place was taken by official glorification of premarital chastity, and of the sanctity of marriage. Abortion was prohibited. The liberty of divorce was radically curtailed; by the decree of 14 July 1944, it was made impossible for the vast majority of citizens. Soviet Russia today has a more monogamous, stable, and Victorian family and marriage life than do most Western countries.

"Considering that the whole cycle occurred under a single regime, the experiment is highly informative. It clearly shows the destructive consequences of unlimited sex freedom, especially in regard to creative growth of culture and civilization."

A system of restraint and terror can help to produce a spectacular change in the morals of the nation and create the expansive energy necessary for a state with an aggressive policy. But to develop the productive energy which is the vital force of a creative civilization, it is only the living sacrifice, the voluntary discipline that each person freely accepts which counts.

The extraordinary challenge of the modern world to the new generation forces them to re-think completely the doubtful way of life of their parents' generation. The energy created by sexual discipline is the driving force which can show us very clearly the aim to pursue and the means of realizing it. Chastity before marriage and fidelity in marriage are the only foundations on which the political, economic and social structure of a new society can be built.

Frank Buchman used to say that the line in the verse, "Make and keep me pure within," contains the greatest words in the English language. As a matter of fact, they are the secret of civilization.

CONRAD HUNTE *of Barbados, Vice-Captain of the world champion West Indies Cricket Team, is one of the most popular sporting figures in the British Commonwealth with its seven hundred million people for whom cricket is a national game. A brilliant opening batsman, he was awarded the Nunes Trophy as "most outstanding player" when West Indies defeated Australia in the 1965 international Test Match series. Hunte believes that sport should serve the larger interests of society, and is much in demand as a speaker on world issues. Recently addressing an African youth conference in Nairobi, Kenya, he declared, "The heart of the race question everywhere is whether change will come through compulsion, leading to dictatorship by one color or another, or by consent based on a God-given liberty that is character-centered and color-blind." Conrad Hunte, 33, was Director of Athletics at Mackinac.*

12

VOICE FROM THE CARIBBEAN

by

Conrad Hunte

COLUMBUS sailed into the Caribbean in 1492 and discovered a
new world. He found here the American Indians, the South
American Indians, and the Caribbean Indians. Thousands from
old Europe followed the path of Columbus. So you have a melting
pot—every class, every race, every culture, every creed. It could
be glorious. It could also be—-and is—dynamite.

The Caribbean forms a natural basin of island stepping-stones.
It stretches from Florida in the United States right down 2,000
miles to the South American mainland, and from Barbados in the
East 1,000 miles to Panama in the West. It includes French, Dutch
and British Guiana, the Republics of Venezuela and Colombia, and
the Central American Republics. It also includes Haiti and the
Dominican Republic, two of the oldest republics in the Western
Hemisphere, the Castro-Soviet regime on Cuba, Puerto Rico with
its close links to the United States, the newly independent British
Commonwealth Dominion of Jamaica, Trinidad and the English-
speaking West Indies, a number of French and Dutch island territories, and the legendary resort islets of the Bahamas and the
Antilles.

I asked the Scandinavians what they hear about the Caribbean.
The answer was immediate—"Cuba." I asked the Japanese the
same thing. Again one word, "Cuba." Many believe it is inevitable
that Cuba's voice represents the Caribbean—and that it will represent the future of Latin America as well. I don't. I believe in
a new voice from the Caribbean.

The twenty million people of the Caribbean are fast-moving and
very revolution-conscious. Like the rest of the world, we face three

choices—the atomization of man, the Communization of man, or the modernization of man.

It is not easy to think of the possibility of atomic fallout when you are lying on the white, sandy beaches of the blue Caribbean, with the sound of calypso in your ears and the sip of alcohol on your lips. But it is a possibility we need to face. That is the first choice.

The second possibility is the Communization of man. A basic Caribbean industry is sugar, on which great numbers depend for their livelihood, and from Communist Cuba has come a plan to wreck the sugar industry. In St. Vincent, due to successful strikes and sabotage, it has been destroyed. Also this year there has been a wave of strikes in the sugar plantations of Jamaica, with sugar workers agitating for more and more wages and less and less work. Production of sugar has gone down, and sugar producers do not know what to do.

This situation is directly linked to British Guiana in the South where you had last year a strike of 53 days, with 170 killed, 800 badly wounded, and 1600 homes totally destroyed. So throughout one of our staple industries you have upheaval and turmoil.

What about oil—the other most important factor in the Caribbean economy? There is Venezuela, a prime producer of oil, where tight military and police measures have been taken to prevent riots and sabotage. Soldiers guard the bridges with machine guns. Yet many feel the situation is getting worse.

Trinidad is another producer of oil. There a small force of Chinese-trained Communists are determined to stop at nothing in order to make Communism the policy of Trinidad and the Caribbean.

But I believe there's a third choice. I believe that the real alternative for us in the Caribbean is the modernization of man. And I want to describe to you some of the positive actions of this last year alone.

In British Guiana you have a population of 683,000. More than half of them are Indians—Indian Indians—who came over the seas at the turn of the century or earlier and have made British Guiana their home. Then you've got the Africans who came earlier still. They are second in terms of population. Then you've got the third group, the Europeans, and other minorities.

One year ago Dr. Cheddy Jagan was Prime Minister, and he worked closely with Fidel Castro and people from China and

Russia. He lost the election last November. During that time, of course, there was the ferment and unrest I described earlier—all part of their campaign to take over. They had people in the forests trained with Cuban weapons to seize the country physically the moment Jagan got back in. So you might say that by Divine Providence this nation was kept open to the right ideology, though it may not be for long.

At the moment in British Guiana all doors are open to Moral Re-Armament. I went down there with Mr. Chris Schutz, who was a research officer with the South African Government and is now giving his full time to Moral Re-Armament. We met with the Governor and the Prime Minister, Forbes Burnham, and leaders of the business world.

The Prime Minister urged us to launch an all-out action program for British Guiana. He told us of the remarkable impact of MRA films in his capital city of Georgetown. *The Crowning Experience,* for instance, dramatizing a new dimension in race relations in the American South and distributed by Universal Pictures, Inc., topped all attendance records including those of favorites like *Ben Hur* and *The Ten Commandments.* Documentaries like *Which Way America?* and the Congolese Army film *You Can Count On Us,* have also proved popular in many private institutions and with the Armed Forces.

Government leaders in British Guiana look to Mackinac with great hope. Some of you ought to answer their appeal and come and work there, not only for the sake of saving this country which the Communists hope to make their entry point onto the Latin American mainland, but because it is one way into the Dominican Republic, into Vietnam and into China. The Prime Minister hopes you will come soon.

You will find there a vigorous force of youth. They are of every ethnic group. They are taking the program of Moral Re-Armament from school to school, college to college and into the sugar and bauxite industries. As you know, if you fight on the right issues you soon find out where and who the enemy is. In their own schools the students uncovered a hornet's nest of subversive elements. These elements went to the principal and said, "We would like to have a debate on the subject, 'Can Moral Re-Armament answer the problems of British Guiana?' "

The problems are clear—too much drink, too much sex, division and bitterness of every kind. The hall was packed and six staff members were judges. At the end the MRA-trained youth won an overwhelming victory.

This, of course, made headlines and the businessmen got interested. We put to them that we needed $800 (B.W.I.) per person to bring a delegation to Mackinac for training. One businessman said to me, "This is the effective way to deal with our country and give it an answer. I would like to play my part. Here is the fare for one delegate and $500 a year for three years." If you can get money out of businessmen you have started something.

At this point the Governor picked up the ball. He is a South African by birth, working with the British Foreign Service, and has real vision for British Guiana. He had me stay in his home and arranged a private conference there for some of the top businessmen and youth. He showed them our films. They were fascinated. At the end these men themselves took on the task of raising all funds needed to send the entire Guianese delegation to Mackinac.

Just south of Cuba is the island of Jamaica where a Caribbean Conference was held earlier this year. The conference, attended by 150 youth from all over the area, was opened by the Governor General, Sir Clifford Campbell. He said, "This is an epoch-making event not only for Jamaica and the Caribbean, but for the world." Out of that conference came a nucleus of youth who set to work in the sugar plantations, in the schools and with the businessmen of the country.

Here is one typical story showing their impact on our major national problem of laziness. A post office worker had gone to his boss previously and said, "Please sir, can I have time to go home and rest? I am feeling ill." The boss being a kind man, like most Jamaicans, gave him permission. But he didn't go home at all. He went to the cinema with his girl friend. At the conference he realized that wasn't playing ball, so he went back to his boss and said, "I'm sorry, sir. I've been dishonest and lazy, please forgive me." The boss did so, and gave him added responsibilities.

What part do sportsmen have in modernizing man? What are we living for? The West Indies cricket team are now champions of the world and we have just soundly licked Australia. People say that cricketers are heroes to their friends and their fans, but hypocrites to themselves and their families. I'm afraid that is true. I know from my own experience that I used to talk way up there and live way down here. I did not have a goal in life that could include everybody—black, white, brown and yellow.

When I met Moral Re-Armament they did not take me on an intellectual exercise. They simply presented me with absolute moral standards. And I had to admit I did not get to first base on them. So I decided to correct certain simple points like being honest with my father, and paying back money to my West Indies Cricket Board of Control for stacking my expense accounts. Then I had to apologize to my headmaster not only for cheating in examinations at school, which is common, but for taking money out of school funds, while Student-Body President, to use for myself.

I put these things right as a start. Then I decided to draw a battleline in our cricket team as we went around the world. Naturally if you fight, you'll get opposition. It is healthy. And some of the people in my own team and on the Board decided to oppose me. It wasn't easy, but I stuck it out.

I faced a real choice. I had been Vice-Captain for two years and had my heart set on becoming Captain. I was not chosen. I was bitter. I wanted to chuck cricket. This would have greatly weakened our team. I faced the question whether to sacrifice my country's standing in sports for my own personal aim of becoming Captain, or whether to sacrifice my selfishness so my country might enhance its cricket reputation and also give something unique, apart from cricket, to the Commonwealth and the world. Finally I chose the latter.

In the Port-of-Spain, Trinidad, towards the end of the last match, the wicket was not very good. My teammates found it difficult to cope with, but my own training in Moral Re-Armament helped me to adapt. Putting aside the joy of hitting sixes and fours so that everybody could cheer, I decided to stick it out and keep going whatever happened. The result was I was out there from beginning to end of the match, with my teammates falling around me like ripe apples off a tree. After one particularly easy out, a voice from the crowd shouted, "Hunte, why don't you teach your teammates Moral Re-Armament?"

S. Douglas Cornell, Ph.D., *physicist and President of Mackinac College, spent his early career as a scientific warfare adviser at the heart of the military establishment in Washington. He received his B.A. and Ph.D. degrees at Yale University, worked four years as a development engineer with the Eastman Kodak Company, and following service in World War II as a Naval Commander, headed the Planning Division of the Research and Development Board of the Department of Defense, leaving this post in 1952 to become for thirteen years Executive Officer of the National Academy of Sciences. He resigned in 1965 to take up his post at Mackinac College. Dr. Cornell is 50 years old, and has two sons and two daughters.*

13

NEW FRONTIER IN
EDUCATION

by

S. Douglas Cornell

B Y TRAINING I am a physicist. First employed as an engineer-physicist in industry, I then spent ten years on military weapons development—four of those years as a naval officer in World War II, the next six in the top levels of the research and development organization of the Department of Defense.

Those years taught me what enormous military power science has given to the United States of America. I am proud of having had the chance to play a small part in the building of that power. They also taught me that military power in a nuclear age is no answer to the world's problems; it can ultimately do no more than buy us time while the answer is found in other ways.

The dilemma of science and technology in the mid-twentieth century is this: They have led to world-shaking developments that must be exploited if humanity is to be served; and they have led to world-wide illusions that must be corrected if humanity is to be saved.

Technology advances. Military power grows, while military security diminishes. National affluence reaches an all-time high, and so do adult crime and juvenile delinquency. Leisure time multiplies, and so do all the diseases of stress, mental ills and alcoholism. The Pill makes it easy to become a nation of smaller, more affluent, and, we say, more stable families; but it leads to premarital indulgence on such a scale that multitudes of young people become quite unfit for the responsibilities of marriage.

Science penetrates into the depths of nature—the course of the galaxies through space and time, the intricate structure of matter, the ways in which nature replicates herself, the roots and determinants of life itself. To the unwary these triumphs of the intellect create the illusion that life and nature are purely mechanistic, that there is no moral truth, no absolute right or wrong, no law except the laws of mathematics. This is the most dangerous illusion of all. For to destroy the sense of right and wrong, in the name of creating what we choose to call a wholly "rational" man, is a fraud on our civilization and our culture. Such a man will not solve the problems of our time.

In a series of lectures at the University of Missouri, Edward Teller said, "The danger is Man. Nothing can save us except the powers of reason and morality in Man himself." Professor Teller is right. Many people say the same thing. Reason and morality: the trouble is that when we deal with the problem, we work on the first prong and not on the second. I did myself until a few years ago when two new elements entered my life: a basic purpose commensurate with the dangers and challenges in the world of science, and a set of moral standards to guide me in following that purpose.

Professor Teller recognizes this issue in his lectures. Having lived, as he says, for a quarter of a century with the Atomic Age, and the problems of increasing human power, he sees the threat of Communism. He believes that the Communists may succeed in establishing world empire because they have a world aim and are ruthless in following it.

His point of view is that the facts of technology demand some plan for a united world and, he says, the Communists "stand ready to heed the call of history." Then he says:

"Let us look at ourselves. Are we ready? In 1945 the United States was considered the country to which all people of the world looked with confidence, often with gratitude and, without exception, with admiration. In 1945 it was clear that the twentieth century is the American century. What have we done in the last two decades? Our standard of living that had been the highest in the world went up by another 50 per cent. Our safety went down by more than that amount. And the respect has in many quarters turned to ridicule. There is something wrong with what we are doing. The main thing that is wrong with our way of leading the world is aimlessness."

To achieve unity seems impossible, Professor Teller says. "There is no precedent in the history of the world for this kind of change. How could we expect agreement between people basically different in tradition, in language, in their way of life, in everything that counts? We want to find a way of cooperation and equality between the yellow, the brown, the black and the white races. We want to find a peaceful way in which feudal and tribal societies can adapt themselves to the demands of our century."

If we had a thousand years to do this job, Teller says, it still would not be enough. "If freedom is to survive," he says, "it will be by a miracle—the miracle that millions of free and independent human beings can in fact perform." Then he says, "We should establish world order by the slow and safe process of evolution, but we don't have the time. It must be done by a revolution."

I learned this same lesson when in the course of my duties in Washington, I would sit with the Joint Chiefs of Staff, or with the senior research and development officials of the Department of Defense. They were dedicated, highly trained, hard working, brilliant individuals; but they didn't know how to unite on the toughest problems. The result was that the really difficult problems were rarely solved by the people who knew the most about them—because they couldn't agree. Such problems usually had to be passed up to the next level, and ultimately they were dealt with by people who knew very much less about them.

The central problem of our times is not the technical or scientific problem, but the moral problem. We have had an industrial revolution and an intellectual revolution. Each has had its revolutionaries. Now the true wave of the future is the moral revolution. The problem is to develop modern man at a pace to match the development of modern science. The problem is to build the men who will be guided by God to guide the nations.

Four months ago I was asked to accept the presidency of Mackinac College. I had not the slightest interest in becoming president of a college. I held what I believe to be the best job that a scientist-administrator can have in this country—at the heart of the nation's foremost scientific institution. It is a job that is far better in every way I can think of than a college presidency—no faculty to deal with, no students, no troublesome Board of Trustees, no money-raising, and an excellent salary. Why did I decide to leave it? Because what I was really being asked to do was to join with revolutionary men and women in creating a center of revolution for the equipping of revolutionaries. On any lesser basis I had no interest whatever. A friend asked me, "Will this college operate on the principles of Moral Re-Armament?" I said, "Of course; otherwise there would be no point in founding it."

Mackinac College will be formed and governed by men and women who understand two things that institutions of higher education appear often to forget—that knowledge is power, and that the way in which power is used is as important as the power itself.

Any system of higher education that confers such power without looking at the same time to questions of character and moral quality is dangerously irresponsible. Such an educational system is on the road to becoming not a prop and safeguard of democracy but a menace to it. Mackinac College will be dedicated to a pioneer role in equipping men and women to face and solve the towering problems of the years that lie ahead.

Thomas Jefferson said the function of education in a democracy is to transmit anew to each generation the best of the intellectual and moral heritage of the past. The first part of that dictum is assiduously pursued by every college and university. The second is more and more ignored because it is a pesky, prickly thing that is even hard to define, especially for those who are fuzzy about it in their own lives and don't like moral absolutes.

Higher education has in these last years in this country more and more failed to meet a vital need of democracy—God's requirement of a firm and clear moral framework for policy and action—a framework that must be explicitly, deliberately erected in men's lives. The aim of Mackinac College will be to produce men and women with perceptions awakened to the deepest needs of the world, with trained minds, staunch spirits, and sure direction. Men and women who recognize the eternal verities not as historical curiosities, but as determinants of the rise and fall of civilizations. Men and women with the fullest opportunity to find the reality and the adventure of God's governance in their lives. Men and women with the mental capacity, the physical health, and the moral equipment to meet and master the problems of the modern age.

Students can expect of Mackinac College determined devotion to that aim. Mackinac College will expect of its students the will to learn and the will to be responsible.

The need of the age is for responsible men who look to the power of the living God to advance His kingdom on earth. Such men will bring light in darkness, sense in folly, inspiration in confusion.

I do not have the historian's gift, but I do know this: unless we now put our ideology straight and our priorities right, we are headed for a dark age in the history of human freedom. Science and technology will not save us. Only a restored sense of purpose and a restored sense of sin can lead to a restored sense of hope. The tide of history can run either way. The choice and the challenge lie before us, each one. We *can* build a new world. Mackinac College will be committed to that task.

JØRGEN THYGESEN *of Denmark is a member of a Jutland farming family who for centuries have been leaders in Danish agriculture. His grandfather founded the Farm Employers Association. After serving in the Resistance movement against the German occupation during World War II, he left Copenhagen University to join the re-established Danish Army after the war and was commissioned an officer in the Armored Corps. Versed in seven languages, he has specialized in the history of ideological movements in Europe and their implications for international affairs today. "It is one thing," he said in a recent interview, "for the West to export the institutions of democracy. It is another to transmit the spirit and way of life from which they spring, and which alone can make them work." Mr. Thygesen is 40 years old. He and his wife make their home in Copenhagen.*

14

EUROPE NEEDS AN IDEOLOGY

by

Jørgen Thygesen

TWENTY YEARS ago this year, just about the time most of you were born, my country was liberated by British and American troops after five dark years of German occupation. While we fought in the underground—or Resistance—we eagerly, secretly tuned our radios to follow every advance of the American, French and British armies. Europe was shattered and in ruins. But the troops that crossed our borders were received jubilantly as heroes and saviors.

We are 340 million people in Western Europe, 87 million in Eastern Europe, and 223 million in the Soviet Union west of the Urals—altogether 650 million on the continent.

From these old lands of genius and conflict, of ancient culture and gas-chamber cruelty have come Fascism, Nazism, Communism, Imperialism—and the greatest ideals of liberty and freedom for mankind.

We are amongst the most highly educated, skilled, literate and industrious peoples on earth. Yet, with all our modern civilization, we seem to have brought destruction and division not only to ourselves, but to the world. Truly we need a modernization of man if Europe is to fulfill her role in history.

I come from the Nordic North, the area that stretches from Canada and the North Pole to the Russian frontier, from Greenland, Iceland, Norway, Sweden to Finland in the East and Denmark in the South. The English-speaking people generally call us Scandinavia. There are about 20 million of us.

Most of you may know that it was the Vikings from the North who first discovered America in the year 1000. But unfortunately

Leif Ericsson, who made the discovery, reported back that it was only rocks and sea, so no tourist trade was developed at the time.

Other Vikings went East and founded Moscow, others again ruled England, plundered France, robbed the Spanish coast and became imperial guards in Constantinople. But for the last couple of centuries we have lived smugly in our corner of Europe and let the world go by—that is, until the Second World War caught up with us and made it clear that no one can live smugly in a corner any more.

However, some of the old fighting spirit of the Vikings is still left. During the war while Sweden remained neutral, Norway and Denmark fought Germany, and Finland fought Russia singlehanded in 1939-40, winning the admiration of the entire world.

Now let us look at Western Europe as it was in 1945, exhausted by the war. Three major factors contributed to its rapid reconstruction.

1. Marshall aid—the billions of dollars that America poured into our economy, having already spilled the blood of her sons for our sake.

2. The North Atlantic Treaty Organization (NATO)—the pact of common defense between U.S.A., Canada, and most of the West European countries which provided us with a shield against Stalin's threat of take-over.

3. The statesmanship of West Germany's Chancellor Konrad Adenauer, France's Premier and Foreign Minister Robert Schuman, and Italy's Premier Alcide de Gasperi.

Adenauer, Schuman and de Gasperi, inspired by their common teacher the great Italian philosopher Don Sturzo, all knew Moral Re-Armament. Don Sturzo called it "Fire from Heaven." Schuman and Adenauer who both came to its European headquarters at Caux, Switzerland, laid the foundation of the new Europe with a reconciliation of the age-old enemies Germany and France. They credited MRA with being a decisive factor in the work for a new Europe. The governments of both nations decorated Dr. Buchman in recognition of this fact.

Schuman said: "If MRA were just another movement, I would not be interested. But it is a world-wide transformation of human society."

Chancellor Adenauer said that MRA was "the unseen spirit behind recent successfully concluded negotiations," referring to the Coal-Steel Agreement which was the cornerstone of the Schuman

Plan and of what is today called the Common Market of Europe.

These men and others like them had an ideology. They had an aim far beyond themselves, their nations, even beyond Europe. They worked for a new world. Therefore they succeeded in uniting where there was division, healing where there was hate, and out of their work sprang the fruit and miracle of economic recovery and the massive rebuilding of a continent.

Today men mistake this fruit for the roots. They concentrate on economic gain and higher living standards, and the result is self-interests that clash and plans that are stifled.

They appeal to old nationalisms in hope of greatness, and find the devils of division that led to disaster rising again. There are still those who believe we can divide the Communist bloc that way, and there are those who equally foolishly believe that Eastern Europe can be bought by higher living standards, washing machines, refrigerators and cars.

What is really needed is the root of the answer that was brought to Europe right after the war—the ideology of freedom, from which springs the fruit of economic progress, true patriotism and unity within and between nations.

Many had diagnosed the illness of our age. Some had formulated answers. But no one like Frank Buchman had raised a force of men and women across the world trained to apply the principles of freedom to the crises of the day.

In 1946 Dr. Buchman arrived in Europe, and at the first World Assembly for Moral Re-Armament at Caux, Switzerland he immediately set to work reconciling the enemy nations of Europe. Within a short time, through the good offices of General Lucius D. Clay, then Commander of the American Zone of Occupation, the first Germans to leave their country after the war were given special passports and permission to come to Caux. Among them were Dr. Konrad Adenauer and Dr. Heinrich Lübke who is today President of Germany, and as the years went by the first hundreds were followed by ten thousand Germans, miners, officers, political leaders. It was, said President Eugen Gerstenmaier of the German Senate, a welcoming back of Germany into the family of nations.

Among those to meet the Germans were many who had been tortured in concentration camps and lost their families and possessions in the war, and who naturally blamed Germany for all their sufferings.

Among these was a Frenchwoman, Madame Irene Laure. She

was President of the three million Socialist women of France, a Deputy to the French National Assembly from Marseille, and leader of the Resistance in Southern France. Her son had been tortured by the Gestapo.

When she heard Germans were present she packed her bags and wanted to leave. But Buchman said to her, "As a Socialist you work for equality and brotherhood—what kind of Europe are you going to build without the Germans?" Madame Laure stayed, thought it over, asked to speak. From the platform she told how she had wanted to see all Germany destroyed, and enjoyed the bombings of the cities. She asked the Germans to forgive her for her hatred, because with hatred no new world would be built, but division and war perpetuated.

Now imagine the Germans sitting there—expecting to be charged with the whole guilt of the war, and super-defensive against any accusation. And here comes this leading woman from France who apologizes to them. Of course all defenses melted like ice in the sun and the spontaneous reaction was—no, no, not you; it is us, it is we who must ask forgiveness.

Mme. Laure then spoke on the radio to the whole German people, in state after state to each local government, and in Berlin at the time of the airlift. And German after German spoke in France at big and small gatherings, committing their lives to build a new Europe.

This work of reconciliation reached to my own nation, Denmark. An officer of the German General Staff who had planned the occupation of our country, and later met Moral Re-Armament, spoke to a mass meeting in Copenhagen—front page news across the country—asking the whole nation not to forget but to forgive and undertake a common commitment to rebuild the world. In this way German after German spoke in Holland, Belgium, Britain and France dedicating themselves honestly and unselfishly to creating a new Europe.

So the friendship and trust created personally between the leaders, and between statesmen like Adenauer and Schuman, was cemented between the peoples of the cities and lands that had fought each other so bitterly.

Recently Norwegian Prime Minister Einar Gerhardsen, who himself suffered in a concentration camp under the Nazis, went on the first state visit to Germany after the war. As always there are people who want to perpetuate old divisions, and certain newspapermen asked Mr. Gerhardsen, "What did you feel when you were received in Bonn by an honor-guard of German soldiers with the helmets you recognized from your own time in concentration camp?" Replied the Prime Minister, "I did not see the helmets. I looked these young men straight in the eyes, and I saw a new Germany."

Since the war our countries in Northern Europe have achieved living standards that are amongst the highest in the world. We have no unemployment, health insurance from cradle to grave, and old-age pensions for every citizen.

But here is what Social-Democratic Swedish Prime Minister Tage Erlander said recently:

"We suffer from an inflation of neuroses, of restlessness, anxiety and depression. People seem to get nothing out of life, everything seems senseless to them. The social standard in Sweden is outstanding, and yet our society has not become a happy society."

Isn't that curious? Here we have all we could want in the world —and still we are not happy.

The reason is that freedom is betrayed through concepts such as "free love," "free speech," and "free to do as you please." The prophets of these shibboleths borrow the word "free" because it is the most precious of all to us, and make of it a false panacea that results in personal and national license, insurrection and slavery.

Ingmar Bergman, the noted Swedish film producer who a short time ago was awarded Europe's highest cultural prize—the Erasmus Prize of $25,000—remarked when he received the news: "People have been reduced to lust-driven animals." This is the clearest possible statement of where these false freedoms lead us.

But there is a generation rising against this hoax. It is a generation which understands that true freedom has to be bought and fought for in each of us and in each generation. That only those are truly free who are bound always to fight for what they know to be right regardless of popularity, success or comfort. Young men and women who stand for the honesty essential to any free society built on trust; for the straight living and unselfish care required to create a prejudice-free world with enough for all.

You have over a hundred of this new European generation at this Demonstration. They are typical of the new Europe which wants to be involved. They are ready to go with you to the ends of the earth to make the vision of a new world come true.

BREMER HOFMEYR *of Pretoria, a noted athlete and
student of African affairs, comes from a distinguished South African family who in recent years
have held seven Cabinet posts. His cousin, J. H.
Hofmeyr was Field Marshal Smuts' closest political colleague. A Rhodes Scholar who played for
Oxford at Rugby and Tennis, Hofmeyr also holds
degrees from the University of South Africa and
Cambridge University where he captained Trinity
Hall at cricket. Since 1934, as one of Dr. Buchman's early associates, he has pioneered throughout his home continent a fresh approach to the
embittered issues of race and ideology. He is a
friend of national leaders in 26 African countries,
and has spoken and written widely in Europe,
Asia, and the Americas. Mr. Hofmeyr, 56, is
married to the former Agnes Leakey of Kenya.
They have two sons.*

15

CONTINENT OF THE FUTURE

by

Bremer Hofmeyr

I WANT to take you into a fascinating continent—one which grips the heart of everyone who once visits it. It is the continent of Africa. It is five times as large as the United States. It has mighty rivers which first enabled the explorers who could not cut their way through tropical rain forests to penetrate into the interior. It has a system of great lakes like North America. One of them, Lake Victoria, is larger than Lake Michigan or Lake Huron which we see from Mackinac Island. There is the great Sahara desert. In its heart lie the ruins of Roman cities and petrified trees. So once it was fertile. Perhaps man's greed denuded it. And perhaps man's imaginative use of science will make it blossom again. There is high plateau country. In Kenya and Ethiopia men farm at 9,000 feet altitude. There are eternally snow-capped mountains right on the equator. Mount Kilimanjaro in Tanganyika is over 19,000 feet, yet it is normal for parties of school children in good training to scale it without mountaineering equipment.

Vast portions of Africa were until comparatively recently isolated from the outside world. The source of the Nile was a matter of furious debate and unknown to Europe until just over 100 years ago. Then a man, Speke, found that it tumbled out of Lake Victoria over the Owen Falls, a huge full-blown river at its start. The pool beneath the falls was thick with fish that had climbed the river thus far and could go no further, except an occasional giant that negotiated the falls like a powerful salmon. These falls have disappeared in a giant hydro-electric scheme at Jinja, and the Nile in this modern age starts its 2,000 mile journey by turning huge turbines. But the fishermen are still to be seen below. That is the

White Nile. The other Nile, the Blue Nile, rises also from a lake, Lake Tana in Ethiopia and they meet in the Sudan at Khartoum. Whether one is wholly white, and one wholly blue is open to dispute. But certainly a long way below Khartoum you can still see that the two sides of the river bear waters of different color.

Much of Africa was so isolated from the rest of the world that when European exploration penetrated the interior, the wheel was unknown. Yet Africa has had civilizations that are lost in history. On the Congo-Rwanda border the remains of an adding mechanism was found that betokened developments long forgotten. In Rhodesia you have the mysterious Zimbabwe ruins. Everything is oval, whereas everything in later African architecture is round.

Freedom has come like a hurricane to Africa. In the last eight years some 35 countries have got their independence. Britain, France, Germany, Spain, Portugal, Holland, Belgium, Italy, the Scandinavian countries all had their finger in the colonial pie. If the Scandinavians seem surprised at this, remember that the castle where the President of Ghana lives, where the colonial governors resided, had its slave dungeons with grated exits to the waiting slave ships, and was called Christiansborg Castle. Africa is full of surprises. You land in Liberia to find that the national flag is the Stars and Stripes, and the Liberian currency is the U.S. dollar.

It is always a mistake to impose the American or European connotation of words on to Africa. Freedom in Africa is a passion. It means the freedom of a people to run their affairs their way without intereference.

It certainly does not mean copying Western Democracy. The two party system is not taking root in Africa. The one party state is rapidly becoming the pattern. And in some countries like Kenya it is true to say that the change has not come by the compulsion of the party in power, but by the belief of those who did not win the elections that it is the natural way to govern. President Nyerere, in an article, claims that the one party state is not necessarily undemocratic. He points to the traditional pattern of African tribal rule where the Chief listens to the views of all the elders and then summarizes their view in his own statement which is then law. The elders, Nyerere points out, are not in two parties, but the system is not undemocratic. The difference, of course, is that a modern state is much larger and does not have the homogenous nature of the ancient tribe. Time will show. And the other factor is the modern army which has the ability to assume power if it so decides.

106

If Europe or America want to help Africa foster freedom and democracy, and they cannot transpose their two-party forms, what can they do? The answer is simple. They can live and help Africa live Moral Re-Armament. Because country after country that has been asking European governments to leave, has been welcoming any man of any color who truly lives as a remaker of the world, above racialism, nationalism and personal self-interest; who has been ready to change his own life, to put right what is wrong, and has the care and imagination to enter the lives of other men and build sound, incorruptible, patriotic leadership. If recent African history teaches one thing above all, it is that a nation morally rearmed will preserve its freedom. That is why one may truly say that Moral Re-Armament is the ideology of freedom.

The independent African countries (apart from South Africa) are all represented in the O.A.U. (the Organization of African Unity). But there are certain major groups within it. You have the Muslim North including the Mediterranean countries from Egypt to Morocco, the countries bordering the Sahara, and also the northern parts of Ghana and Nigeria which are Muslim with the majority power in Nigeria lying with the Muslims. These countries like Nigeria with Muslim and non-Muslim have deep divisions. The Northerners in Nigeria are very conscious of their age-old culture and tend to feel superior to the Southerners. The Southerners feel that they are the progressives and superior to the Northerners whom they regard as reactionary.

Then there is the big French-speaking community of nations, and they are a very important group. Many of them feel differently towards France than former British subjects feel towards Britain. France tried to administer what was once its overseas territories as a part of France. It was "Overseas France." African representatives sat in the French Chamber of Deputies. A man like Mr. Houphouet-Boigny sat in practically every French Cabinet for years before independence. And I believe that emotionally many still feel something about France that a Nigerian leader does not feel about Britain. Leopold Senghor, the President of Senegal, is a noted French poet, who is read not only in his country but in France.

These countries have their own organization, the OCAM, the Communal Organization of Africa and Malagasy. Malagasy is what used to be called Madagascar. They move with the African organizations, but insist on being separately mentioned. They are in fact partly African and partly Polynesian and their appearance is distinctive. Their President is an unusual man, Mr. Tsiranana. He is very outspoken and always ready to drop a bombshell in discussions when he feels things are getting unreal. In Cairo, when one man after another got up to attack Mr. Tshombe of the Congo, Tsiranana got to his microphone. He had not come to Cairo to defend Mr. Tshombe, he said, but people were speaking as though he were the devil incarnate and would certainly go to hell. For all he knew this might be Tshombe's fate, but he ventured to say that if Tshombe landed in hell he would probably find a lot of the present company there too.

Many of these French-speaking African leaders have had long contact with Moral Re-Armament. They have been to our center in Paris. They have us as their official guests. There are many open doors. It is important because this group, the OCAM, may play a major part in the development of freedom in Africa.

Then there is the area of white minority rule in the South— South Africa, South-West Africa, Rhodesia, Angola and Mocambique. I, myself, am from South Africa. The man who first made the word "apartheid" current was Dr. Malan. My mother's brother, Dr. Bremer, was his Minister of Health. But our home is in the heart of Johannesburg. We run it for everyone. We have conferences for all races. We believe that it is only as men of all races take up their task of rebuilding the world that they will find unity and the right political, social and economic set-up. We have had plays with all races in the cast presenting the ideas of Moral Re-Armament through drama. We took such a play into Stellenbosch, the university where five out of the six South African Prime Ministers were educated, where Dr. Verwoerd was a professor and where his children study. The Mayor welcomed the cast on the stage of the Town Hall. The students stayed over an hour to talk with the Africans in the cast. For many of them it was a wholly new experience in their lives.

One of the most helpful developments in the daily life of the Africans in the great cities is the revolution in housing. Johannesburg was notorious for its slums and its "shanty-towns." These have disappeared and today there is a vast city of 600,000 inhabitants. There are four-room, brick cottages with waterborne sewage and fenced gardens with flowers, vegetable gardens and fruit trees. The houses are simple, but create the possibility of a life of dignity.

The pioneering work was done by a man who met Moral Re-

Armament, yielded the certainty that he knew what was best, and began to listen to God. He got the idea for large-scale housing developments, training the Africans who had not the opportunity until then of entering the skilled building trades, and producing houses that would rent for two to three pounds—six to nine dollars a month. He invited the City Council of Johannesburg to see the first sod moved and then to see the first families moving in. His work became a pattern for the nation.

I believe that we are going to see revolutionary changes in South Africa. They will come by vision or by violence. As I move around Africa I am struck by the colossal need for almost every skill, educational, social, economic, agricultural and industrial. I see in South Africa a reservoir of these skills. I long for the day when we in South Africa will say, "Let's forget about what we call self-preservation as our policy. Let us make our national aim to help Africa develop for the good of all men, so that everyone may enjoy the blessings of food and work and freedom and faith." It will be a new aim and we will have to find the new policies to achieve it. For myself I believe the word, "He that seeketh to save his life shall lose it, and he that loseth his life for My sake shall find it." If that word is true, then our greatest security lies in the aim I have outlined.

Adjoining South Africa are three territories that will be much in the news in the coming years. They are the British Protectorates of Basutoland, Bechuanaland and Swaziland. Their economy is tied to that of South Africa. They have a common currency. Basutoland is entirely surrounded by territory of the Republic of South Africa. Swaziland is between South Africa and the Portuguese territory of Moçambique. Bechuanaland is bounded by South Africa, Rhodesia, South West Africa and a small part of Zambia. It is this small border that makes it the escape route for South African refugees. The total population of the three protectorates is just over a million. In the next year or two they will get their independence, and to become viable and truly independent is going to present great problems. But these million people will have three votes in the United Nations.

I wish there were time to speak about the leaders of the new Africa. But I will mention a few. President Kaunda of Zambia rules a key country. The vast mineral resources of Northern Zambia adjoin the wealth of Katanga to form one great treasure chest. This huge mineral basin is the biggest prize in Africa. It includes uranium, copper, zinc, cobalt, titanium and other rare metals. Some are crucial in high temperature jet engines.

I will tell you one little incident about President Kaunda. During the colonial rule he went into a butcher's shop. At the head of the queue was an African. A white man came in and pushed himself to the head of the line. Kaunda walked out in wrath and decided he would never eat meat until the country was independent. Nor did he. It was not a propaganda point. He did not publicise his decision. But it indicates to me an inner conviction and resolution that is deeper than personal interest.

President Kenyatta of Kenya is a remarkable man. He has declared his intention to build a state in which race is not the issue and where all Kenya citizens will have equal opportunity, regardless of color. He has been as good as his word. If he and his associates carry this through unswervingly it will be a mighty challenge to the lands of white minority rule in the South who say a non-racial society in Africa is a dream. He has brought to statesmanship another factor—the belief that the moral life of the citizens is the concern of the ruler of the nation. In great mass meetings he has fearlessly tackled stealing, jealousy, division, drunkenness, womanising. Many leaders around the world might take note.

President Nyerere of Tanzania is a man of infinite goodwill. There is no question about his desire to do the right thing for his country. The question is whether he will be strong enough to withstand some very ruthless forces ranged against him. At heart he is an educator. His recreational interest is translating Shakespeare into Swahili.

The Sudan is in a bitter struggle between the North and the South. The North is Arabic, the South is Bantu. The North is Muslim, the South is Christian or animist. The Minister of the Interior is 30 years old—Sayed Ahmed El Mahdi. He has attended a conference here at Mackinac. He is taking bold initiative to create unity.

What then are the issues before Africa?

The first is still the issue of freedom. Will those countries that are not free become free, and will those that are independent preserve their freedom? China casts longing eyes at Africa. There is the cobalt she needs to become a nuclear power. There are the minerals she needs to become an industrial power. There is the agricultural potential to feed hundreds of millions more if science is imaginatively applied. And there is the room she covets for her population. For in China with less than one third the area of

Africa there are three times as many people.

Then the West is trading heavily in Africa and corruption is reaching gigantic proportions. A bribe of ten per cent to the Minister or the Party is becoming more and more accepted. The Africans blame the Europeans and Americans for bringing corruption. The Europeans and Americans say that they would rather not give bribes, but they are in Africa and it is the African way. In my view those who give bribes and those who receive them have much the same thing in their hearts. But it is certain that this will spell the death of freedom if it goes on. The masses of Africa who are in many cases little better off materially than before independence, see this going on and they will rise up in wrath if it does not stop.

Then also Africa is looking at the East and the West. And this is certain. The claims of the West to be a Christian civilization will be judged not by the words of the religious leaders, but by the actions of the business and commercial firms who operate there. Suppose the West were actually morally rearmed? She could carry to Africa the standards and integrity that would ensure freedom and progress.

There is the eternal war against poverty, ignorance and disease. In Tanzania the average income is 4% of the average American income. In the vast central belt of Africa 10% of the people are educated. In the Nile valley nearly everyone has bilharzia. If this could be eradicated the human energy could be doubled. There is a huge job to be done.

Finally there is the question of what Africa is going to give to the world. It is unthinkable to me that in the mind of God there is not some distinctive thing that this awakening continent is meant to give to the nations at this hour of crisis. I will only speak of one thing that always strikes me in Africa. It is the closeness of the unseen world. President Senghor of Senegal maintains that whether the African is Christian, Muslim or animist, he is never an atheist. Certainly everywhere I have been in Africa—and I have been in 26 countries—I have found it is completely normal to say, "Let us be quiet and listen to God." It does not need a lot of explanation and argument. I wonder if it is not in this realm that Africa's unique gift may lie: to redress the balance of a civilization of swollen heads and shrunken hearts—to restore heart-power, humor and humanity, and to restore the knowledge that the realities that shape man's destiny are not what his hands can handle, but the things that are perceived in his heart and spirit.

111

PIERRE SPOERRI *of Switzerland, a leading authority on communist trends in Eastern Europe, was educated at the Universities of Geneva and Zurich where his father was for many years Rector. He has traveled widely in the Americas, and his ten years in Asia and the Middle East included service in Japan and Korea, Vietnam, Ceylon, Egypt, and two years with Rajmohan Gandhi in India and Pakistan. A Director of the Caux Foundation, he is currently European correspondent of the Indian political weekly* Himmat. *M. Spoerri is 37. He and his wife live in Zurich.*

16

THROUGH THE IRON CURTAIN

by

Pierre Spoerri

VIETNAM today is the most obvious place where the struggle between East and West is being decided. But the fight inside the Communist world, in the hearts and minds of the younger generation of the countries of Eastern Europe and Russia—and eventually China—could be as decisive a battlefield.

In July we had 22 students from Communist Poland in one of our homes in Zurich. We showed them the film of Rajmohan Gandhi's action in India, and followed it with an hour and a half's discussion. The leader of the Polish group was a woman Professor of Metallurgy about five feet tall. She watched with eagle eye all that her flock were doing and saying, and every member of the delegation had to report to that woman every day after breakfast so she would be sure none had run away.

The discussion with these Polish Communists was most interesting. At two points during the evening a wave of laughter went through the group. One was when, in the film, Indian students were seen burning pornographic literature. The Poles seemed to understand that, and it struck me how quickly they saw the relation between moral standards and the reconstruction of a nation. It was clear they were not living more moral lives than people from the West, but they grasped the significance of that point instantly.

The other place where they reacted was when we told how Rajmohan Gandhi himself had changed on the point of corruption, and how in his student days he had tried to corrupt the bus drivers of India's capital, New Delhi. We quoted Gandhi's own story: "I gave the bus driver ten cents and kept ten cents for myself. That is practical socialism." They enjoyed that point immensely.

Many people in the Communist nations today don't believe any more that Communism will create a new world. It is evident to them that selfishness, corruption and greed exist in Russia even 48 years after the Communist revolution which was supposed to usher in a new society. This fact is the Achilles heel of Communism today, and every sincere Communist has to admit that the practice in his country does not correspond to the Marxist theory on which it is supposed to be based.

The tragedy, however, is that just at the moment when the Communist world discovers its own weakness and looks for some new form of moral basis on which to reconstruct its society, the Western world is falling more and more for the so-called "New Morality"— for the worship of sex and material progress. So while the professed materialists of the Communist world begin to seek for spiritual truth, the so-called Christian West is on the point of discarding the very spiritual truth on which its society has been built, and the very weapon with which it could most effectively influence the Communist world.

A Polish writer, Czeslaw Milosz, recently made a penetrating observation: "What goes on in the heads of the Western masses? Have the people of the West lost all faith? What can the West then offer to us? Freedom *from* something is a great deal, but it is not enough. It is much less than freedom *for* something."

A Russian basketball team visited Western Germany last year and a German friend of mine who speaks fluent Russian was asked to look after them. They were tall fellows and didn't look at all like the religious type. So my friend was amazed when after a couple of days two of the Russians came to him and asked, "What does God mean to you?" He answered in a straight-forward way. Then the Russians said, "We were brought up as atheists, but our elders drummed atheism so constantly into our heads that we became convinced there must be something to God after all. So we wanted to come to the West and see for ourselves. But if you walk through an ordinary Western city there is not much evidence of God."

Not all of us will have the chance of penetrating immediately either to Eastern Europe or to Red China, but we may well find ourselves face to face tomorrow with a Communist in our own country or in some other country of the West. The following story happened in the German Ruhr, the industrial heart of Europe.

114

A Moral Re-Armament play was invited to a small mining town just after the war. There were no hotels, so the whole cast was put up in homes.

At that time 72 percent of the seats on the Works Councils of the steel and coal-mining industries of the Ruhr were held by Communists. A young Norwegian of the cast was assigned to the home of a man named Max Bladeck, a coal miner for 30 years and for 22 years a Communist. As soon as the Norwegian entered his home, Bladeck tackled him on the question of Communism. Bladeck refused to come himself to see the MRA play, but as a trained Communist he had to know what was going on and who would be there.

So he sent his daughter to spy.

That was where he made his big mistake! His daughter came home after the show and said: "Father, I have hated you for the last ten years because outside our home you make big speeches about freedom, equality and the end of exploitation, but at home you exploit my mother, you are always at war with the neighbors, and you are a dictator with us children. I saw something in that Moral Re-Armament play that could transform our family and this whole society."

Even if you have been a Communist for 22 years such words from your daughter will shake you.

After that Bladeck saw more and more of us. He didn't believe in God. But after a few days he tried the experiment of listening. He didn't call it listening to God; he called it listening to his better self. We said to him, "It doesn't matter what you *call* it; the main point is that you *do* it." He didn't believe in absolute moral standards, but he admitted that even a Communist society would be better off if you had people living absolute honesty, purity, unselfishness and love.

I won't tell you the whole fascinating story of Max Bladeck. But within a few months a dozen of the top leaders of the West German Communist Party became so convinced of Moral Rearmament that they left the Party. The whole West German Communist hierarchy had to be reorganized. Bladeck's family and home life were transformed. At the next Works Council elections, Bladeck and all his friends were re-elected because the workers now had greater confidence in them. Within four years the number of Communists in the Works Councils of the Ruhr decreased from 72 per cent to 8 per cent.

115

Not long after his first encounter with MRA in the Ruhr, Bladeck was invited by Dr. Frank Buchman to go with him to India. While working in that country he got word of the sudden death of his father and mother back in Germany. As a Communist he had not been to Church since his youth. Now he started to go again to Mass, and soon afterwards he told the priest, "I never believed it would be possible, but I have once more found a real faith in God."

On Bladeck's return to Germany the Communists had a plan for him. They knew he had been a heavy drinker before meeting Moral Re-Armament, so they invited him for an evening on the town. They teased him about his decision to give up liquor. "Oh, you have become holy holy—why not just one little glass?" Finally he gave in. After the first little glass came a second, and a third, and a fourth. And when he didn't know what he was doing any more they put a woman in front of him, the wife of a friend of his, and he didn't know what he was doing with her.

Next morning the story was all over town, and Bladeck was so ashamed that he wrote his friend Frank Buchman not to come and visit him any more. Buchman wired back: "Man-like it is to fall in sin. Fiend-like it is to dwell therein. God-like it is from sin to rise. I have faith in a new Max. Yours loyally, Frank." That telegram transformed Bladeck's life and he has been fighting ever since.

There are several ways we can all help to win the people of the Communist world.

First is by the way we live, wherever we are, and the way we strive to change every man, Communist and non-Communist alike, in all our countries.

The question of discipline plays a very important part in all this. Peter Howard used to tell the story of the young Chinese Communists who now work in Rangoon, Burma and whom he saw in action there. Burma is a Buddhist country, and in order to win Burmese Buddhists the young Chinese stopped drinking, stopped smoking, didn't fool around with women, were at work sharp at 7:30 every morning, and even in the damp heat of that climate always dressed as if they were on parade. By nature, of course, these Chinese young men and women were no better than any others. But their ideology came before their inclinations and this discipline impressed the Burmese. None of the Western representatives in Burma had a passion for their ideas that matched the dedication of the Chinese.

Another way we can penetrate the East is through the theatre.

Communist diplomats in Western capitals often make a point now of attending Moral Re-Armament plays and films. When we gave a play in West Berlin recently we arranged that tickets could be paid for in East German currency. It was estimated that fully one-third of the audience had come from East Germany.

We had one unknown but effective ally on an East German Communist newspaper. He ran a long feature article attacking the play from beginning to end. But at the end of the article he wrote, "This MRA play can be seen in such-and-such a theatre, on such-and-such a date, at such-and-such an hour." That was the only way he could publicize it. It was very effective.

When you saw these people from Communist Europe you saw how hungry they were. They would take the MRA books, tear off the covers, stuff the pages into their clothes, and carry them home like that. Others came week after week for one day to West Berlin, learned the MRA books by heart, then returned and went from house to house passing on to their friends what they had learned.

It has been suggested that the U.S. Government ought to send plays like *Sing-Out '65* to Moscow as part of the Soviet-American Cultural Exchange Program. Nothing could be more effective. Some of you have seen Peter Howard's play *Through the Garden Wall* which will have its French premiere in Paris this autumn. When this play was shown in Rome, many top Italian Communists came to see it. They were so impressed that they had the Communist Labor Unions buy out an entire performance. And in town after town the workers and leftist trade unions did the same. The Communist newspaper *Unita* wrote, "In his own country Mr. Howard is known as the leading exponent of the theatre for creating peace. He lives up to the neck in reality. Everywhere the workers respond to this theatre's appeal. It is a popular play—a popular success."

What most intrigued and challenged Party members about *Through the Garden Wall* was that there surges through it a greater passion to change the world than they themselves possess. Another thing that fascinated them was the personality and identity of the remarkable Jewish physician "Dr. Gold." After the play heated discussions went on among the Communists over this question. One asked, "Does 'Dr. Gold' represent Time?" To which another replied, "Of course not, his action is much faster and more radical than Time."

117

One Communist official was overheard complaining to a trade union leader, "God has come in through the back door of the Communist headquarters. It's just not fair."

When this play was shown in Trieste on the border of Yugoslavia, high Yugoslav officials asked if a tour through Yugoslavia could not be undertaken. It did not prove possible at that time, but it was promised that something would be arranged later.

Should not the French version of this same play be offered by President de Gaulle to all his new friends in Eastern Europe? The President of France recently received the Chiefs of State of Eastern Europe. Would it not be the most natural thing for him to say to them, "This is what we would like to offer you as a cultural exchange." A country like Roumania is steeped in the French language and French culture. I cannot imagine a finer example of French culture for President de Gaulle to offer that country.

The same could be done by the German and Austrian Governments with the German version of Peter Howard's play *Mr. Brown Comes Down the Hill,* opening in Munich in October. Again the cultural agreements with several Eastern countries would make it difficult for their governments to refuse such an offer.

Chancellor Klaus, who is head of the Austrian Government and has attended conferences at Mackinac, said recently that it was through Peter Howard and Moral Re-Armament that he had learned to speak in an effective way to the leaders of the Communist countries. He might be just the man to undertake such a program.

Plays alone, of course, will not do it. Only personal conviction and passion can turn the tide in the war of ideas. But plays with the right ideology are a unique weapon.

I often recall our first visit to Hokkaido University in Japan with Howard's musical *Space Is So Startling.* Though the play had been officially invited to the university, half an hour before the curtain only a dozen tickets had been sold because leftist students had given the order not to attend. With Communists, however, you have one great advantage. They always have to know what is going on. Three of the Communist leaders came to see Peter Howard and Rajmohan Gandhi before the play, and tried to shock them by exclaiming loudly, "We are for total revolution."

Howard answered them, "We too are for total revolution."

The students continued, "We think Mr. Khrushchev and Mr.

Mao Tse-tung are not revolutionary enough."

Howard replied, "We too think that Mr. Khrushchev and Mr. Mao Tse-tung are not revolutionary enough." And he pursued the point saying, "Any revolution that does not deal with selfishness, hate and greed is completely out of date in an atomic age. Why do you insist on having such out-moded ideas?"

The leftist students had never heard such language before. They rescinded their directive, and quickly passed around the order to the students to attend the show. The auditorium was packed, and afterwards vigorous discussions went on till early morning.

I am convinced that the Communist world may be as open, if not more open, to a new revolutionary way of life than the countries of the West. Most of these men and women have already fought and sacrificed for their revolution. But many have been disillusioned. If we can now give them the chance to participate in the true revolution of morally re-arming the world, they could be the decisive force in ushering in a new era for the entire human race.

JOHN A. SAYRE, *former Varsity stroke at the University of Washington, rowed in the coxwainless four that won a Gold Medal at the Rome Olympics of 1960. His crews also took a Gold Medal at the Pan American Games of 1959, and defeated the Russians at Moscow in 1958. Last year, with "Rusty" Wailes, he was invited by the President of the U.S. Olympic Committee to help train the American squad in preparation for the Tokyo Games. The* NEWSLETTER, *organ of the U.S. Olympic Committee, paid tribute to their work as "one of the great contributions to the Tokyo success story." Sayre and Wailes have spoken on over 100 U.S. campuses from the University of California at Berkeley to the Air Force and Naval Academies. John Sayre was Co-Director of the 1965 Mackinac Demonstration. He is 29 years old, married, with three children.*

17

WHAT MAKES
A REVOLUTIONARY

by

John Sayre

WHAT IS the element in our lives as young Americans that is going to make us different from other Americans who have gone into Vietnam, Santo Domingo and other world hot spots? What is the element that is going to make us modern? What is the element that is going to make us revolutionary?

Four years ago I came to this conference on Mackinac Island. It was mid-winter. I had been here three days and was fed to the teeth with people telling me I ought to be different. The truth was nobody had told me that, but suddenly a conscience I had buried for several years was brought back to life. And I had to face the very simple places in my life I needed to straighten out.

I took steps to put right some of them. It had an immediate effect in straightening out my marriage and helping to straighten out a number of other things. So I was convinced that Moral Re-Armament actually worked on a personal level. But I didn't yet know whether it was an idea relevant to a world that was being torn apart by hate, anarchy, and violence of every kind.

The Japanese students who had rioted against General Eisenhower in Tokyo, and whom you saw in their film the other night, were in America at the time. These men put on their play *The Tiger*. I saw it in Miami with "Rusty" Wailes. It convinced me.

Then a Brazilian General invited "Rusty" and me to come to Latin America with this play. We accepted because I wanted to see whether this idea could actually work on a national scale. So I went to Brazil, green as grass, wet behind the ears, not knowing much of anything but like most young Americans thinking I did.

We went to Recife in Northeastern Brazil—a riot-torn city where a few weeks earlier Government troops had been herding students back into the university at bayonet point, and cruisers in the harbor had their guns turned on the city. The Brazilian Government, supported by the military, asked this force of Moral Re-Armament to see if we could bring an answer to Recife.

I remember boarding the plane in Rio de Janeiro to fly north. I was scared stiff because Americans are not popular in South America, and when I walk about down there it is not difficult to mistake me for a North American. As we got on the plane an Air Force officer said, "We will certainly fly you to Recife, but we can take no responsibility for your safety after you get there."

We went into Recife and put on the play. There was a tumultuous response. Pretty soon the theatre could not hold the crowds and we had to move to the football stadiums where 50, 60 and 70 thousand people a night came to see it.

The night I specially remember was when we went to a place outside Recife called "Little Moscow." It is almost 90 percent Communist. The Mayor, the City Council, the leading citizens are Communists. It is a workers city and a tough one.

We went out there to show a film. Just before the film began there was a tropical cloud-burst, and when it rains down there it really rains. It rained for two hours. But over 500 Communists stood in this rain watching an MRA film.

As soon as the film was over I was eager to get out of the rain and was rushing down a side street with a young Frenchman who spoke Portuguese. Suddenly out of the dark sprang eight young men. They backed my friend and me up against the wall and said, "We have just seen your film. We are Communists. We believe Fidel Castro has the only answer for Latin America, but we are interested in the idea portrayed in this film. What does Moral Re-Armament mean to you as an American?"

There I stood in the rain with my back to the wall, facing eight very tough cookies. And believe me I did not know what to say. All I knew was that some great intellectual argument wasn't going to be worth a hill of beans.

I was a man who said he believed in God and never paid much attention to Him. But here was one point in my life where I said under my breath, "God, if you have something for me to say let me know what it is."

The only thought I got was to tell these young Communists how I had to change. So I told them how I had competed against the

Russians in the Olympics, how I had seen the passion and conviction of those Soviet Communists, and how I had become convinced then that anti-Communism alone was no answer to their challenge.

I told them how about this time I met a man who was trained in the ideas of Moral Re-Armament. He was from Finland. He came up to me and said, "Sayre, you know the greatest reactionaries in the world today are the people who want to see the world different, or another race, class or person different, but aren't willing to be different themselves." He said, "The most logical place to start, if you want to see the world different, is with yourself." He said, "We in Europe believe that absolute moral standards have got to be the basis of a free society, if free men are going to keep their freedom."

Having just graduated from the University of Washington I laughed and said, "Absolute moral standards! That's absolute nonsense." However, I knew this wasn't quite true, as a standard had to be absolute or it was no standard.

I told these young Communists how this man from Finland challenged me to the revolutionary experiment of facing my life against four absolute standards and seeing where I needed to be different. I told them how I took absolute honesty and said, "All right Sayre, you complain about corruption in government, you complain about the dishonesty in your own family and among your friends, but if you decided to get absolutely honest yourself, where would you need to start?"

Immediately I got some very clear thoughts that took absolute moral standards out of the realm of idealism and brought them down to earth with a very hard, cold, practical thump. I realized that for two years, while I had been making these big speeches in the universities and high schools, I had been cheating the government on my income tax.

The young Brazilian Communists stared at me unbelievingly. Then I said, "I complained about corruption in government, but when I went through University I used to cheat in my exams."

You know if you cheat yourself you have very little to say to men like Bobby Baker. The Brazilians didn't know about Bobby Baker, but they suddenly began to look at each other sheepishly, and then burst out laughing. They said, "You know, we were all rioting in the streets two weeks ago against the corruption in our state government. But we all cheat to get through the universities here. So from what you have just said, we can't have much to offer to our own politicians." Then they said, "What else did you have to do?"

I told them how at the University of Washington I used to have a Volkswagen. There were two things I had to do about that Volkswagen. Number one, I had to get honest about the several hundred dollars worth of parking tickets I owed to the campus cops. Number two, when I was a senior I was quite well known at the university, being stroke of the Varsity Crew. But what most people didn't know was that I came within an ace of never getting on that Varsity Crew and never graduating from university.

One night I had been out in my Volkswagen and had a bit too much to drink. It was three o'clock in the morning, and I had another fellow in the car with me. He was tight and under 21. For some reason we were driving up and down the steps of the university library. I grant you that is an odd place to be with a Volkswagen, and the campus cops thought the same thing when they came along. A guardian angel must have been protecting me because I had put a pillowcase over my license plate.

Suddenly the campus cops appeared and I took off. They came after me and I went tearing down the street and they kept trying to pass me. Every time they tried to pass I would pull in front of them. All the time I kept thinking, "Boy, I'm getting in deeper and deeper."

I came to a corner where there was a big concrete viaduct that goes down the hill. I came roaring around this corner and then realized the policemen, because they had a big Ford, could go much faster than I could. They went zipping by and tried to run me into the concrete viaduct. I still don't know how I did it, but I jammed on the brakes, spun the wheel, and the Volkswagen instead of going over the viaduct turned around in a flash and went back up the hill. The cops in their Ford could not turn around fast enough, so I roared up to the back of my fraternity house, drove into the backyard, buried my Volkswagen in a heap of dry leaves, and didn't drive it for two weeks.

At this point the young Brazilian Communists were rolling on the ground with laughter.

I told them how one of the things I had to put straight was to go back to the campus police and see what the charges were against me and my Volkswagen. I told them how scared I was, but that by this time I had met Moral Re-Armament and decided to put my own life in order so I could give something in terms of leadership to my nation.

I told them how I had gone to the police and reminded them of the green Volkswagen of two years before. The Police Supervisor stared, then called somebody on the phone and in came a huge cop six foot six and about 250 pounds. He was one of the roughest characters I had ever seen. The Supervisor said, "Tell your story to this man."

I repeated my story and the cop's eyes widened. Finally he said, "I was the man who chased you that night. If I had caught you I would have killed you."

I said, "I haven't come in here just to ease my conscience, but because I want to give a new leadership to America and help equip her to give a new leadership to the world. To do that I have to put right certain things, and this is one. Are there any charges against me?" They looked at me and said, "There are no charges."

Then the police asked me all about Moral Re-Armament and what we wanted to do in the world. They said, "What you have done today has given us more hope for this country than anything we have seen in years. You have answered the cynicism we have built up through watching how young America talks high and mighty and lives pretty low and dirty."

This story hit the Brazilians. They said, "We attack the police, but of course we are guilty of everything we accuse them of."

Then I told them very simply the points in my own life which I had had to put straight. One of them was to get honest with my wife, which is far more difficult than winning a gold medal in the Olympics. I told them how I said to a friend, "I can't get absolutely honest with my wife. It will kill her." My friend replied, "Women don't die that easily." And he added, "Besides you are just a coward," which was true. I told them how I had a straight talk with my wife and she said at the end, "I suspected those things but now for the first time I feel I can trust you." She in turn was honest with me, and it changed our marriage.

The Communists were really riveted by this story. Then I went on to tell them how I had to stop certain wrong relationships, habits and thoughts. I told them how I had to apologize to various people I hated and was jealous of.

I told them of a man who was a friend of mine but had inherited a big oil company when he was 24. He had bought a big house, yacht and sports car and began to treat his old friends, of whom I was one, very snobbishly. I am a proud man and I reacted to that. We got into a fight at a cocktail party, and I threw this man in the flower bed because I weighed 50 pounds more than he did.

As a result he hated me and I hated him.

I had the very clear thought, "This man treated you wrongly, but your hatred is wrong. Go to him and apologize for it."

I walked into this man's office and said, "Jim, I have been jealous of you for the last year because of the money you inherited. I have told stories behind your back. I have hated your guts and I am sorry. Will you please forgive me?"

This man, normally cocky and arrogant and always right, for the first time in my memory was speechless. He stood up and said, "John, what you have just said took more guts than anything I ever did in my life. The truth is I have been more wrong than you. Will you forgive me?" He changed.

That night Jim asked me to dinner at his house. He said, "You are different, perhaps you can help me. I have an older brother and we haven't spoken for three months. He is getting married next month and hasn't invited me to the wedding. How can I get united with my brother?" I said, "Well, we can try the simple experiment of listening to the voice within your heart—call it God, conscience or whatever you want—that can actually tell you what you ought to do with your life, what you ought to fight for in your nation, what you ought to fight for in the world. And you might also get an idea how to put things right with your brother."

We sat for five minutes in silence in this man's living room. At the end he said, "I had the thought to call my brother, ask him for lunch and tell him over lunch that I hated him since we were kids because I always thought my father preferred him to me. In every-thing I did I set out to beat my brother. I beat him in sports, I beat him in school, I beat him in business, and he hates me for it. I thought to tell my brother not where he is wrong, but where I have been wrong, and ask his forgiveness."

The man did this with his brother, and they were united.

By this time I realized we had been talking over an hour, and these eight young Communists were standing there spellbound. I went on to tell them the things I had had to put right when I made amends to my professors about cheating, how I had to get honest with my parents, how I had to pay for text books stolen from the college book store. Finally they said, "You are the first American we have ever met who had the courage to be honest about himself and his country. If there were many Americans like you in Brazil today Castro wouldn't have a chance."

126

They continued, "What you are talking about is revolution. We see it is a greater revolution than what Castro has offered us. It means we have actually got to make people different. And we see it is far more difficult to make people different than to shoot them. We see that the corruption and selfishness we have accused the capitalists and the Americans of, we are guilty of ourselves. And that if we are going to build anything different in Brazil, in Latin America or in the world, we are first going to have to take these steps you have told us about. If there are men like you from North America that we can work with and fight with, perhaps together we can create permanent justice, equality and freedom for all men."

The root of most of these young men's hatred against society was their hatred against someone in their own family. Many were illegitimate, and they hated the father they may never have known. That was the root of their hate.

They began to get clear on this. They began to get a cure for it, and many of these young Communists and their Party colleagues went back to the Catholic Church and found again a relevant faith. When President Quadros of Brazil resigned in 1961, and the Communists called for bloody revolution, former Communists like these in Recife refused to respond to the call for violence, saying that Moral Re-Armament had shown them a far bigger revolution.

This is the revolutionary quality—the ability to change human nature—that we need as young Americans. It is the quality that we could take into Vietnam, into Latin America, into Africa. We need to give and must give military aid, economic aid and social aid to these countries. But we can and must give them also an answer to the hate, corruption, selfishness and impurity that divides and destroys their nation and robs them of greatness.

What the world really wants from America is an answer to the hunger in the hearts of men. If we can give them that, the world will come running.

PETER HOWARD, *world leader of Moral Re-Armament from the death of Frank Buchman in 1961 to his own in Lima, Peru, in February, 1965 during a Latin American tour, closed last year's Mackinac Island Conference with the following address. In it he refers to the plan for this year's Demonstration which was largely the result of his own burning conviction for American youth. Born in London, graduate of Oxford, Howard captained England at Rugby football and became leading political columnist for Lord Beaverbrook's* EXPRESS *newspapers. His fifteen books sold over four million copies in a dozen languages. He was author of seventeen plays which on stage and in films have been seen in most countries of the free world and on both sides of the Iron Curtain. Twenty-seven heads of government sent messages to his widow, the former Wimbledon tennis champion Doris Metaxa. President Belaunde Terry of Peru directed that his body lie in state in the City Hall of Lima.*

18

TODAY'S PAUL REVERES

by

Peter Howard

I WANT to thank every single one of the delegates to this Assembly. When we started, I said that age had much to learn from youth. Only the most stubborn, selfish, senile could have lived through this Assembly and not learned great lessons in life from young people who have been here. Perhaps many of you have things to learn. But those of us older people who have not had some great, growing experiences of God have missed the miracle.

I don't go for this talk of leaving. It's for the grasshoppers. We never need leave each other. We are bound by the steel bands of a common revolutionary task. Anybody who wants to leave can leave, but the rest of us can stick together as one force in a growing world family "till kingdom come."

There was a man called Paul Revere and he rode, and in spirit certain people rode with him. The great majority did not. Some of them never left their wives, their beds, their comforts and their corn. Some turned back. But the people who built the nation and who are remembered by history were the men who rode. And you are going out today like so many Paul Reveres.

Don't be a bit disconcerted if not everybody rides with you. They won't. Don't be a bit disconcerted if some people get the collywobbles when the bullets fly. They will. But the people who ride and keep on riding are going to make a permanent mark on the history of this country and on the story of liberty.

Since George Washington I don't know when any group of Americans have set forth to serve this country, determined to finance their revolution on their knees. It's extremely healthy and you're going to do it.

If I had medals for you all, I'd give every one of you a medal. I don't have medals. And I don't think you would want them if I had. But you're going to the places where you could earn them.

I hope you will run into the heaviest kind of artillery. If you find artillery firing, you know you're on target. And don't be confused by it one bit. If you live in West Virginia, which is a glorious place, and if you heave a rock out of the window and a dog starts howling, you can be sure you've hit something. And if I were you, I'd just keep on heaving the rocks.

You've all got plans, haven't you? Does the United States of America have plans? Do all the plans of the United States of America work? Why not? I won't puzzle you. This is not a contest morning. Of course, the plans are enormously important, and your imagination and dare can shift this country. But no plan will ever work unless it is backed by convinced, disciplined people. And that is what impresses me so much about most of you. You have caught the vision of a revolutionized America and a revolutionized world. You are ready to back it with the discipline of your lives. That is what counts.

You ought to be so different when you go back home that your own dog, if you have a dog, bites you. A lot of you are. But some of you are not. I say to those who have just a few more hours of battle preparation before you go where the bullets fly: big doors swing on little hinges. Remember that. Sometimes the hinge on which a big door swings is just about the size of a cigarette, sometimes it may be a relationship, sometimes a habit. Sometimes that hinge is just that 5 or 10 percent that we still hang onto.

I'll say one thing from my own knowledge. If you have a 5 or 10 percent which you still hang onto, that is what runs your life. The thing we hang onto and will not give is the thing that runs us.

We have had very clear diagnosis in this assembly of the world situation. But some people diagnose for years and they never bring a cure. There was a man I was fond of when I worked in newspapers. And the comradeship of the press is one of the finest kinds of comradeship on earth outside of Moral Re-Armament. I was devoted to this man and we spent ten years diagnosing him. It's what some people do for the troubles of America or the free world.

This man's problem was very simple. He was a Christian and he drank too much. He was too fond of women. He spent money he hadn't got and his home was hell. I tried to help him. I used to give him money because I had a lot in those days. I used to give him one drink about six o'clock at night and then bring him back into the office. Of course, as soon as I'd said goodbye, he'd go out and have six more drinks.

Diagnosis, perfect. We all knew his problems. Nobody brought a cure.

The very day that I attended to the hinges in my own life on which big doors swung—they were quite simple, paying back money I'd stolen, getting straight with my wife and children, facing my arrogance as an Englishman—that man came up to me in the office and said, "I want to talk to you, something has happened to you." He changed. He went back to his church. He got straight about money. And until he died, he was a much loved father and husband.

Diagnosis is one thing, but building an answer that works is another. And a faith to take that answer to the nation is another still. Let anybody criticize Moral Re-Armament who has himself built a force like this to carry an answer to America. If they have done it, let them speak. If they have not done it, let them learn. That's fair enough, isn't it?

The real links—the bridge—between emotion and action are concrete, costly, daily decisions. People who refuse to change will accuse you of emotionalism and a million other things. Don't be fooled by it one minute. It only means that you've got your drill right on the nerve. So keep on drilling. Watch them jump and howl and soon they'll change.

I think we have an answer here. I want to tell you the verdict of two men.

The newspaperman Al Kuettner, head of the Southern civil rights desk of United Press International, has been twice praised, once in *Time* magazine and once in *Newsweek,* as one of the greatest American reporters covering the racial situation. He came up here to Mackinac. He'd just been in Mississippi. He'd just been in Florida. He was sick at heart because he is a decent American. He said at the end of three days, "You have here the answer the whole of America is longing for. And nobody else is giving it to us."

Then there was the actor Sidney Poitier. I quote to you what he said on the telephone from Hollywood two days ago. "I cannot get out of my mind," he said, "that you have the living demonstration America is seeking." That man cares very deeply for humanity.

One thing which I know impressed him, and which has enormously impressed me, is these Indians. That Indian play yesterday troubled me deeply. I'm glad I have been invited to New Mexico. And I want to say again that the Indian people can live and give something to every section of America and the world which no other people can give. There are certain things the white people can do, certain things the colored people can do, but the Indians can speak with absolute authority to both, and they can speak to the world with a voice that has not yet been heard from America. Think how the Asians will listen to you. Think how the Africans will listen to you. Think how the Latin Americans will listen to you. And they're going to listen if you do your job when you get home.

I want to say one last thing, and it is about Communism. A lot of people talk about Communism. But the point statesmen in my country, and I think in America, completely fail to grasp, is this: Every trained Marxist dialectician knows that according to his own belief, either freedom is going to be destroyed, or Marxism is going to be destroyed, or eventually they'll destroy each other.

So, in the mind of a convinced Communist there can be no permanent accord between his idea, and the ideas of liberty and God. In the free world we so hunger for peace that we are willing to come to terms with anybody provided they leave us alone. That's why today Russian socialism is the modern version of that famous agrarian reform movement in China. Do you remember? There was no Communism in China, it was just a great, big agrarian reform. I think the theory started in Britain. You don't like British cooking in America, with some reason, but you sure do swallow British philosophy. And then that great agrarian reformer, Castro, the hero of the peasants, do you remember him? You even unbelted 7 million of your big, capitalist New York dollars to finance Castro—and he skinned you alive.

You had Castro agrarian reform, you had Chinese agrarian reform. Now, heaven help us, you've got Russian socialism as the answer to Chinese Communism. And America is pushing that down the throat of Asia. She's pushing it down the throat of Africa. She's pushing it down the throat of Europe.

Do watch it, because if those are facts, and I believe them to be facts, and if Lenin meant what he said, "We can never succeed until the myth of God is removed from the mind of man," then the only intelligent action for the men who love liberty is to create a revolution bigger than Communism that needs everybody to carry it forward. Then you can say to the Communists, "We want to revolutionize the world. We are going to revolutionize the world. Come and help us do it in the right way."

That is the only synthesis that will get the Marxist out of his dilemma. The Communists know it. That's why Moscow frequently recognizes Moral Re-Armament as the ideology of democracy in the modern world. That is why Peking attacks us so ferociously and says we are the only people they fear. Sooner or later, democracy too will recognize this truth or perish. It could happen both ways— recognition of an answer or destruction from lack of it—sooner than we think, because history is marching at a prodigious pace.

In the next months you in the United States have got to match the revolutionary passion and relentlessness of men determined to take over Latin America, take over Africa, take over Asia—and who are not, repeat not, going to leave this country and Canada to stew in their own juice.

If you interpret this as an attack on Communists, you're wrong. I think Communists for the most part are wholly sincere in their desire to revolutionize the world. What I hate is the self-righteous condescension of men and women in the free world who say they believe in God, but live as if He never existed, and think we can continue our selfish, comfortable, easy-going, divided ways undisturbed. That is modern madness. And I believe you are going out to end it.

19

MACKINAC—KEY TO AMERICA'S WORLD ROLE

An article by Ramakrishna Vaitheswaran in
HIMMAT, *national weekly of India,*
August 26, 1965

THE WORLD has heard a great deal about one side of the U.S.A.
—of Negroes denied civil rights, living in ghettos, subject to
indignities and even brutalities. Occasionally pent-up feelings
channeled by organized groups find expression in riots, street
fighting and even insurrectionary incendiarism and sniping such
as in the Watts district of Los Angeles, which hit world headlines.

But though much may yet be heard of the Negro revolt against
the white man, the struggle for civil rights is already becoming
a thing of the past as leaders like Martin Luther King move into
other arenas of conflict and the NAACP concerns itself increasingly
with raising the status and social standing of the Negro people of
America. Acute social problems such as that of the disintegrating
family, marriage breakups and illegitimate births, which are far
more acute among the Negroes, are being faced more boldly.

A second side of America which all are aware of is her extreme
confidence as a world power able to determine with her strength
and know-how the issues of war and peace, and apt to be irritating
to sensitive Afro-Asians. "We want a friend and not a master,"
said President Ayub Kahn of Pakistan in a national broadcast on
the subject of the deteriorating relations between his country and
America.

But the most significant fact about the U.S.A. is neither the
self-defeating violence of the minority races nor the temporary
frictions of its international policy. For an Asian observer, the
Demonstration at Mackinac Island, Michigan, which is the United
States training center for Moral Re-Armament, holds the key for
the role of America in the world of tomorrow.

The long-suffering and patient American Indian, who hitherto preferred the eloquence of silence to the noise of protest, is conspicuous at this conference by his leadership, untainted by the bitterness of the past and unique in his vision for the whole world. Four hundred Indians from 65 tribes, the largest Indian gathering in recent years, have produced a pageant of American history that is remarkable for its simple grandeur and truthful dignity, its compulsive freedom from hatred and its passionate longing for a world in which there is a place for all men under the Great Creator.

At a time when reports of the violence of aimless youth who beat and burn as a pastime shocks the nation to a sense of crisis, and the drift of the indifferent turns into a demonstration against country and character, thousands of youth from schools and colleges all over the nation find here a fresh challenge in clean living, a new purpose in patriotism and an infectious care for the entire world.

I shall never forget in all my life the welcome which Rajmohan Gandhi, grandson of the Mahatma, and Masahide Shibusawa, great grandson of the founder of modern industrial Japan, received in Mackinac Island on their arrival here—a thousand singing, swinging, purely passionate boys and girls whose only thought for the moment was to express their concern for Asia by doing honor to the Asian leaders. Nor shall I forget the crowds of young men and women who questioned us endlessly because they wanted to help us.

They were ready to pay any price in order to do it and they meant what they said. "We are an explosive generation," they declared. "We want to race to take up the responsibility previous generations have not had the dare to accept."

They declare in a manifesto to the world, "We believe in America. We want a great country—respected and followed because of our great purpose and way of life. Our generation is going to explode the hate, fear and greed that blocks the progress of humanity. We will not remain comfortable and quiet while millions the world over have too little to eat, millions are deprived of their just freedom, and millions in our own country are starved of any purpose for which to live."

One evening a young Negro girl said, quite simply, "I have always been conscious of the white people. I hated them. I realized suddenly today that for many days now I haven't thought about the color of skin—mine or anyone else's." It was as natural as that. This multi-racial family of white, black, brown and Ameri-

135

can Indian felt they needed each other because the task that they had undertaken—to change the entire world—was so big. It is so normal to live like a family and so stupid to be driven by hate that has less and less to justify it as it grows stronger and stronger.

I understood at Mackinac what "modernizing man" meant.

The whole world is here—Asia, Europe, Africa, Latin America and Australia as well as every part of the United States and Canada. They come worried about this nation, perhaps even resentful of her leadership, certainly anxious that they should help this country fulfill her world responsibility better. But, where they anticipate arrogance, they find a ready listener and where they expect resistance, they find response. It comes as a pleasant shock that this country, tired of the aimlessness of affluence, frustrated by the senseless indulgence and wanton destruction of a sick generation, and defeated by the failure to evoke any enthusiasm in the nation or abroad for its world responsibility, is turning to what a friend of mine called "pure undiluted Moral Re-Armament."

Simultaneously with the conference, 150 youth with a magnificent musical called *Sing-Out '65* have been operating on Cape Cod and the prosperous resort areas of the East Coast, winning and changing the influential families of the nation. Task forces have moved out to Washington, D.C., the backward mining areas of Appalachia in West Virginia, and the reservation country of the Southwest. From there they go to the world.

Out of Mackinac has emerged a strategy to win continents such as Asia and Latin America whose leaders have gathered here. Mr. Masahide Shibusawa outlined his strategy as follows:

"The Prime Minister of Korea wants to have a Mackinac type of youth demonstration in Korea this autumn where the youth of the world would come and give the youth there this new theme and new conception of the modernization of man. The leadership of Japan also wants very much to have the best idea planted in the minds of her youth. World conquest is the dream of Peking, and we have got to create a belt of bigger ideas around China."

Inviting young Americans in their hundreds to help us in Asia, Rajmohan Gandhi declared, "Vietnam is extremely important and I thank God for America's presence there, but our aim is far more than the defense of South Asia and the Far East. Our aim is with Moral Re-Armament to capture Peking and Moscow.

"To bring these things about we shall need large sums of money. We should use planes carrying large forces of young Americans,

136

South Americans and Europeans to Asian lands. We shall need plays, and we shall need machines.

"We shall also need a few things far more important than that —brave men and women prepared to take not just a year or two but perhaps five or ten or their whole life to live in and try to change those lands. You will need to learn the secret of modernizing man, of changing the character of men you meet, of making them strong and great, fearless and incorruptible.

"Your job is to fulfill America's mighty destiny to feed, clothe and house the hungry millions of the world far more effectively and far more speedily than the Communists can ever do."

The world came to Mackinac, and from Mackinac is emerging a strategy to change continents—and the people who will do it.

TORCH OF FREEDOM

The following pages summarize in pictures the meteoric course of "Sing-Out '65"—young America's musical spectacular and chief product of Mackinac—across the capitals, campuses and military camps on both sides of the Pacific. This report is from "The Denver Post": "AIR FORCE ACADEMY, COLORADO, NOVEMBER 15—The explosive force of 180 college and high school age Americans from 62 U.S. campuses descended on Arnold Hall Sunday and left a tremendous impact on the lives of some 2,500 Air Force Academy cadets, their dates and a few invited guests from Colorado Springs. The Moral Re-Armament (MRA) traveling hit show 'Sing-Out '65,' was wildly received by an audience that all but filled huge Arnold Hall. So great was the appreciation for the talented performers, the entire audience rose to its feet and cheered through eight encores that followed a stellar, two-hour performance. This new breed of young Americans had the audience electrified from the start with the vitality of their appearance and their voices."

139

20

TORCH OF FREEDOM

*The following address by J. Blanton Belk, Jr. on Labor Day
closed the Demonstration for Modernizing America
and launched "Sing-Out '65" on its world tour.*

SING-OUT '65 is the torch of freedom for this generation all over the world.

If we spread this idea massively enough the world need not be red, or dead. The whole world can be rebuilt. Here you have got a new, tough generation of young Americans, with the commitment to go and do the job.

Twenty-five years ago my generation rose up to put down Nazism and Fascism. And if our freedom is threatened again militarily, believe me we will pick up a gun and fight again militarily.

Nearly two hundred years ago the men who founded this country set out to pattern national unity for the whole world. Those men gave their lives, their fortunes and their sacred honor. Now here is a new generation of Americans going out to do the same thing.

Think of the races together in that play *Sing-Out '65*. Think of the classes together—labor and management. Think of the families united there. What is it going to mean for America to have this going through Asia, through Africa, through Europe, through Latin America? Why, the whole world is going to stand up and cheer. So I want to congratulate the youth. As an old Navy man I would go anywhere in the world with them.

I also want to pay tribute to the parents, because if it wasn't for them we wouldn't have *Sing-Out '65*. This is an American revolution where parents leave their sons and daughters free to find the will of Almighty God and obey it to the ends of the earth. That is America's message to the world. And the world will listen to them because of it.

An ambassador said to me after seeing *Sing-Out '65* in Washington: "This ought to become America's foreign policy." A general from the Joint Chiefs of Staff said, "This is the most unabashed display of patriotism I have ever seen." A nun came to see the show at the World's Fair. She came backstage and told the cast: "You are doing the work of God for America." The great artist Henry Cass who directed this show—the only man Bernard Shaw would trust with his plays—said about *Sing-Out '65:* "This is the happiest expression of what life is all about."

You all know what Stan Musial said. He was one of America's baseball greats, and is Director of President Johnson's physical fitness program. He came up here last month. He said, "You've got the missing factor at Mackinac. Now what it needs is massive multiplication in America."

We want to plan that this morning. We must plan how to multiply massively this idea of Moral Re-Armament from coast to coast, so that America truly becomes the land of the free and the home of the brave.

All Republicans, and even some Democrats, know who Gerald Ford is. He is Minority Leader in the House of Representatives. He spoke here three days ago and paid tribute to what Moral Re-Armament is doing to answer pacifism in America. He said, "The pacifist beatniks here at home worry the boys in Vietnam more than the Viet Cong attacks."

If this is true, then it is also true that America's front line of defense lies in the character and purpose of her people. And *Sing-Out '65,* which creates this character and purpose, is part of America's front line of defense in the world. It is national service of the highest order. It is patriotism of the highest order.

Dr. Konrad Adenauer of Germany has just written about this play. I saw him recently in Bonn. He is 89. He had heard about the impact of *Sing-Out '65* on Washington. He wrote a letter that arrived yesterday:

Dear Mr. Belk:

News has just reached me of a demonstration arranged by Moral Re-Armament in Washington and it made me think back to the meeting we had sometime ago here in my office in Bonn. The reports you gave me then about the situation in the United States made a deep impression upon me. But above all, I have a vivid memory of the final phrase with which you bade me

141

good-bye. You said to me, 'You Germans and Europeans always say Europe needs the United States. But I want to say to you, Dr. Adenauer, that the United States needs Europe.'

Those words of yours came back to me forcibly as public attention at Geneva has again been focused on relations between the United States and Europe. In my opinion America needs Europe not only as a spiritual force in which American civilization had its origins, but also because the security of the United States itself is most vulnerable in Europe. If the Soviet Union were to succeed in reaching the goal for which it has striven for decades, namely to include Europe in its sphere of influence, then the Soviet Union would be by far the strongest power in the world.

Please, therefore, help to see that the United States does not concentrate exclusively on Southeast Asia, but also remembers the importance of Europe. I believe that the conferences which are held in America through Moral Re-Armament will offer good opportunity to work in this direction.

With friendly greetings,

Ever yours,

Konrad Adenauer

Besides Europe, we've had news this morning from Asia and Latin America and Africa. You see, though we in the United States have poured out a lot of material aid around the world—and I thank God we have—ideologically we have been an underdeveloped nation. Now, suddenly, everybody is interested because America is getting an ideology.

Now a new generation stands up out of the heart of this nation and they say, "Freedom isn't free, you've got to sacrifice for your liberty." They are willing to pay any price, undergo any sacrifice, to spread freedom and liberty all over the globe. And I say hurray for them.

They are the new voice of America. And the world will listen to them because their convictions are backed by disciplined, committed lives. The world will listen to them and follow them, and together we can usher in history's greatest age.

SING OUT
STEPS OUT

Young
takes to

Some of the 130-

company of

America the road

strong traveling
"Sing-Out '65"

HENRY CASS, *Director of "Sing-Out '65,"
has had a distinguished career in theatre,
opera, films and television. As producer
to the Old Vic, London, he directed
Shakespeare, including "Julius Caesar,"
"MacBeth," "Richard III," "The Taming
of the Shrew" and "King Lear;" Bernard
Shaw, including "St Joan" and "Major
Barbara;" and a new version of "Peer
Gynt." He produced "Julius Caesar" in
modern dress in 1939, and "Carmen" at
Covent Garden in 1946. Mr. Cass has
since directed several of Peter Howard's
plays at the Westminster, London. He
came to the United States this summer
specially to direct "Sing-Out '65" at the
Mackinac Island Studios.*

*The Colwell Brothers of Hollywood, from left Paul, Ralph and Steve,
authors of the musical "Sing-Out '65," travel the globe with their repertory
of songs in 48 foreign languages. They write music, "not only with the
big beat but with the big idea." Following Asian visit, the trio are leading
their cast of 130 from 62 U.S. campuses on coast-to-coast tour of American colleges and universities.*

Hollywood Bowl crowd of 15,000 gives "Sing-Out '65" a rousing send-off on their Asian tour. Four searchlights over stage represent the four standards of Moral Re-Armament.

5,000 overflow Washington Hilton ballroom for "Sing-Out '65." "I have always hoped," said one diplomat just returned from East Europe, "to see the show-conscious U.S.A. dramatize her traditional values as effectively as the Communists dramatize theirs. Now I have seen it."

Following the Watts riots, Los Angeles County Board of Supervisors requested show for 2,500 high school students of the area, here applauding. Said a Board member, "This spirit is more necessary than federal aid."

Father Forbes of Sophia, Japan's largest Catholic university, thanks the cast on behalf of the President of the University. "It is a magnificent portrayal of an idea and an ideal," he said. 3,000 students crowded into 1,000-seat hall, hung from ceiling girders to get a view.

Students of Waseda University, Tokyo, noted for hostility to Americans, queue for "Sing-Out '65." They gave show roaring ovation and surrounded cast afterwards. "If this is America," they said, "we're for America."

Prime Minister Eisaku Sato of Japan and Mme. Sato visit backstage after performance in Tokyo's Metropolitan Gymnasium attended by the American and Soviet Ambassadors. U.S. Envoy Edwin O. Reischauer and Mrs. Reischauer later hosted the cast in a reception at their Embassy residence.

Korean Prime Minister Chung Il Kwon and family enjoy "Sing-Out" premiere in Seoul. With them is U.S. Ambassador Winthrop G. Brown. Cast were guests of Premier Chung and Korean Businessmen's Association.

Major General Harry J. Sands, Jr. (center), Commander of American U.N. force guarding 38th parallel, and aides lead standing ovation for show in Seoul theatre.

Troops of U.S. 8th Army on 38th parallel see special performance near Panmunjom. Commented a colonel, "You have erased the pacifist image of American youth we have been getting here."

(Left) Brigadier General Robert F. McDermott thanking cast after Air Force Academy performance in Colorado said, "This is the finest show ever presented here." The "Sing-Out" company, who were guests of the Cadet Wing, dined in Mitchell Hall following a tour of the Academy.

(Below) Cadet audience of 2500 were on their feet for half an hour at end of show calling for encore after encore. Said one, "There's never been such enthusiasm except when we beat Army."

WHICH WAY AMERICA?

A LETTER FROM COMBAT INFANTRYMAN JOHN J. HOGAN
(SILVER STAR – POSTHUMOUS) TO HIS FAMILY SHORTLY
BEFORE HE WAS KILLED IN ACTION IN THE PACIFIC –
READ AS PART OF THE FINAL SCENE OF "SING-OUT '65"

I don't know when mail from home has meant so much to me.

As I write the sun is setting on one of those beautiful Pacific days that more than make up for the rainy ones. It's got me thinking about our country.

The American people possess today more power and prestige than any country in the family of nations. Mankind is knocking at our gates, seeking wisdom from our leaders, the hope of peace from our people. Before we can fulfil our destiny to lead the world to sanity and harmony, we shall have to rebuild the fiber of our national life.

Suppose we as a nation find again the faith our fathers knew? Suppose our homes become again the nation's strength, our schools the centers of true learning for good citizenship, our farms and factories the patterns of unity, integrity and national service? Suppose our statesmen learn again to listen to the voice of God? Then we shall know once more the greatness of a nation whose strength is in her obedience to the moral law of God, whose strength is in the spirit of her people.

There is only one other road. Those who divide and conquer, those who would make money and materialism the philosophy of our national life, pride and power the goals of our living, they too have a road to offer and at its end is racial and class warfare and national suicide.

America, choose the right road. Unless there is born again in our people the spirit of sacrifice and service, of moral responsibility, my comrades and I who will fight on the beaches and those of us who will die here will have been exploited and betrayed and fought and died in vain.

It is the eleventh hour. By your choice you will bless or blight mankind for a thousand years to come.

Which road will it be, America?

PACE PUBLICATIONS, 833 SOUTH FLOWER ST., LOS ANGELES, CALIFORNIA

Mayor Milton H. Graham invited "Sing-Out" to Phoenix, Arizona, recently torn by youth riots. 25,000 students in ten city high schools gave show an enthusiastic welcome. Governor Sam Goddard welcomed it to Arizona State Fair.

Mackinac

Where "Sing-Out" Was Born

STAN MUSIAL (r), one of America's all-time baseball greats and Director of the President's Physical Fitness Council, is pictured here with Olympic Gold Medalist John Sayre as they inspect a physical training session at Mackinac Demonstration for Modernizing America. In 22 years of league competition Musial played in 3,026 games, made 3,630 hits, scored 1949 runs, including 475 home runs, and achieved a lifetime batting average of .331. He holds some 50 individual records, few of which are likely to be equalled, and has received greater acclaim for his performance on and off the field than any player in baseball history.

Governor James Hena, Councilman of Tesuque Pueblo, New Mexico, opens Mackinac Demonstration in the name of representatives from 48 Indian tribes who were hosts of the Conference. (Below)

Aerial view of Demonstration Center on Mackinac Island. Buildings will form nucleus of Mackinac College, Michigan's newest, scheduled to open in September, 1966.

1,200 young Americans at Demonstration give exuberant, banner-waving reception to Rajmohan Gandhi, leader of India's youth and chief editor of "Himmat," and Masahide Shibusawa, MRA director in Japan.

(Above) New "Sing-Outs" are springing up in city after city. In Denver, Colorado 150 students from three universities and seven high schools rehearse theme songs from the show— "Up, Up with People" and "Freedom Isn't Free." Meanwhile requests to the original company mount from across the nation and abroad. Governor John Love of Colorado told them, "You are in the tradition of the great fighters for freedom through the centuries."

(Right) Private 1st Class Jack Hogan whose letter home, quoted on opposite page, expresses spirit of dedication of "Sing-Out '65."